INNERSPACE:

A PERSONAL JOURNEY TO HELP AND HEAL

Innerspace: The life force inside my body where my soul exists in combination with physical body.

Inner space: The part of the mind not normally accessible to consciousness.

ISBN 978-0-9958075-0-1

Library and Archives Canada Cataloguing in Publication

Pagana, Tracey, 1957-, author

    Innerspace : a personal journey to help and heal / Tracey Pagana.

ISBN 978-0-9958075-0-1 (softcover)

    1. Pagana, Tracey, 1957-. 2. Healers--Ontario--Biography. 3. Mental healing--Biography. 4. Reiki (Healing system). I. Title.

RZ408.P34A3 2016   615.8'52   C2016-907188-X

Printed in Canada by The Aylmer Express

Tracey can be contacted at: innerspacejourney@gmail.com.

Dedication:

To our Mothers, Chris and Betty:
Believing in someone is magic in motion.

Acknowledgements:

I would like to acknowledge the people in my life starting with the inspirational man I love. Joe, thank you for knowing that I have a calling to which you have been witness; for planting the seed of this book; and for supporting me to the point that you just stand in witness to the flow of purpose as people come and receive what they seem to be searching for; for the answers and the healings required in the moments we share. You are the perfect Gentle Man who is wise and who is polite, supportive, and grounding, as it seems we never know when and where this is going to happen next. With you by my side, I have everything I have ever dreamed come true. I love experiencing, living, every moment, grand or in silence, with you by my side.

To my Editor, to whom I owe this project breath, and flow, and structure. If you spend time with me, you will soon come to know that I have incredible breath control and seldom need to come up for air in a conversation. I have so much passion for the subject matter in this Innerspace journey that I can, at times, barely catch my breath. Susan has been instrumental in so much of this book, and I am so full of an overwhelming spiritual gratitude for her that it brings many emotions to surface. Gratitude and respect, integrity and passion. Susan, I so lovingly call Suze, is an amazing woman full of "Grace and Class." When I first hired her, I remember our first phone conversation ending with, "Tracey, I think you need me and I need you." She has become instrumental in the forming of this project and we are so excited to get it out to the masses of the world around us. She has gone above and beyond what she was initially hired to do. I am humbled she has fallen in love with the messages in these pages and the story I had to share.

I want to thank the many connections I have daily who inspire me with kindness. For example, a co-worker shared the following: "Some people can tell a story and write about it; you just have a story to tell." These acclamations are a part of the journey and a powerful message to all of us. I am so grateful for all your energy and all your understanding and patience, and also for your full acceptance.

I would like to thank our parents, our families, all my teachers, mentors, and the creator of the magical artwork for the cover of this book that allows everyone to see what their own souls call them to claim in the picture. For all the wonderful people who shared their, time, energy, and incredible stories of healing and awareness in the Inter-Connection chapter, thank you. I would like to thank my friend for the beautiful poem explaining something that has become second nature to my being.

I would like to thank every one of you for taking the time to pick up this book. The Universal Energy I was called to write about is alive in these pages. My wish is a simple wish: I wish for everyone to fall in love with themselves and thereby find and befriend their healer within.

From the Editor:

There is a school of thought, referenced in these pages, that says we receive exactly what we need at exactly the right time. When I first connected with Tracey, I had recently retired from my position of 26 years, that being Executive Assistant to a local CEO. I had considered taking on some part-time work in retirement in the area of proofreading and editing and mentioned to a friend that I was eager to get my hands on a manuscript. As it happened, this lady is a good friend of Tracey's and told me she had a friend who was writing a book. She passed my contact information on to Tracey, who contacted me the following day, and, as they say, "The rest is history!"

When I first reviewed Tracey's manuscript, it was obvious Tracey had a story worth telling! Her ability to turn her life around, from one of sadness and heartbreak, despair and addiction, to one of perpetual love and healing and positivity is remarkable! And her willingness to accept guidance and suggestions during the editing stages of preparing her story to be told, as well as her trust and appreciation for my work have been invigorating for me personally.

I am very happy to have been a part of the production of this fascinating story and wish Tracey every success with this project.

Susan Talbot

Foreword:

As I was about to sit down and write this foreword, I was staring out the window and the day was gloomy and quite drab, but I felt my mind filling with happiness and enjoyment. I was perched at the window, looking out at all the different colors of the leaves and watching the squirrels running and hustling with their duties of moving the walnuts to a safe place for the winter. Years ago, I would have never looked beyond the weather; never would have thought beyond my inability or unwillingness to see the good in most things.

A bit about myself: If you are not in the motorcycle industry, I am just a name. I have built several custom motorcycles, travelled all over North America on a motorcycle, and been in many magazines and television shows pertaining to motorcycles. I also run a very successful motorcycle distribution company.

I used to distance myself from the other side of life. I was terrified to open up to someone or to look beyond my own comfort or means. So, I stayed in my safe zone (or in my box) for many years - until the day I met Tracey! Very early on, I told her there was something different about her that I could not put my finger on, but there was definitely something. Over the years with Tracey, and I am proud to say my partner now, she has slowly made me a believer. I can assure you this was not an overnight transformation. I have watched Tracey talk to strangers like she has known them for years. I have seen people just walk up to her and start asking her questions. Going to a grocery store with Tracey is a two- to three-hour trip with the number of people telling me I am a lucky man to have such a wonderful partner. I kept hearing the same comments from many people, and one day, I was overwhelmed with a feeling of happiness and feeling a bit warm. My heart and my mind told me that yes, I am a very lucky man! I have been honoured to hear Tracey sing at Churches. Her voice is extremely calming and very powerful. My emotions pour out, as do the emotions of many others in the pews.

So, after letting my inner space loose, I mentioned to Tracey that I thought she should write a book. I can tell you her first response was not too enthusiastic. However, after four weeks Tracey and I talked again and I was able to convince her of the value of this suggestion. Tracey considered the idea and decided she would attempt to write "just for fun." In actual fact, her ambition and the intensity of this writing project took over Tracey's mind and life for close to a year. Needless to say, the interconnection and watching Tracey's pursuit of her journey and reading her book were overwhelming in a such positive way. I did let my emotions loose and was able to open up and feel the explosive excitement and happiness of reading Innerspace.

Tracey has slowly transformed me into a better person. I am able to use all my senses to their fullest. I see more, I smell more, and I definitely hear more. I can now feel with passion. I allow my hands to feel the inner space of a fellow being.

It's high time we all start treating our "Innerspace" with the utmost respect. Stop fighting your feelings. You will be amazed at how much better you feel and what you can accomplish. Life on earth is about believing you will find warmth and love in everyone. You just have to be nurturing and set examples through acts of kindness. If it could happen to a stubborn man like me, I firmly believe it can and will definitely be obtained and accomplished by every single human in this wonderful world. One way to start this inner space healing is to read this truthful, heartfelt, exciting book.

I am one of the proudest people, along with many others with whom Tracey works closely and personally. We all are extremely happy and excited for Tracey as we witness her consistent climb through her personal struggles and lessons up the steep mountain. She has come to a place in her life where she can rest on a plateau, eventually reaching the peak, in witness to her message of love and caring. Her singular wish is that every person in the world, after reading Innerspace, will get a glimpse of the miracle they were born into and start to fall in love with the person within their own inner space.

Joseph Pagana

Innerspace

"Unique"

What does that word really mean to us? Well, if you were to Google the word or actually look it up in the dictionary, it would suggest sole, single, one of a kind, exclusive, exceptional, and irreplaceable. This sounds simple really, to be "one of a kind." I was watching a Ted Talk speaker recently and she stated in her talk that, statistically, it is suggested your existence is one in four trillion chances of the universe's timing and all the factors it would take to bring your life essence into this human form of existence. Just stop and really think about those statistics: ONE IN FOUR TRILLION CHANCES! Do you know how precious - how rare - you really and truly are?

It has been my experience over the past years working with people and aiding them in becoming aware of the "healer within" that some people choose to remain stagnant in the lives they are living, choosing not to take a peek at what they really want, need, or crave. It has been my experience in this world around me that a rather high percentage of people seem to settle on "simple existence." I am not at all suggesting even for a moment that existing in this state is a judgment of being right or wrong. It is just my personal observation while living among the mass of people to whom I am connected.

The title of this book was not initially my idea. Actually, the name of my book came from the man with whom I share my daily life. He reminds me to be accountable and has encouraged me to write about my journey. I am going to attempt to explain what "innerspace" means to me, as well as try to elaborate on my understanding and experience. The combined word, "inner space" has more of a meaning for me on a soul level. It is the "life force" inside my body, where my soul exists in combination with my birth-given physical body and works as one functioning unit. This soul lives more inside my being and has a knowledge that far surpasses my understanding on a conscious level and is protected in this body in which it lives. My belief is that my human flesh and blood body and my combined experiences in body have come to attain other lessons for my eternal soul in human form. This reality, together and in conjunction, joins as one to my human conscious existence. Therefore, my inner space experience has educated the combined knowledge of both worlds with acute accuracy of who I am and what I am about. This combined presence makes me Tracey Lynn Pagana. I don't like to say "this time around" but I believe I have traveled in many lives and my soul has occupied many bodies, having many different experiences, each time gaining wisdom in the lessons in body and in soul form.

I understand that this way of thinking is my personal experience and my personal gained wisdom. I have also come to know that my soul essence protects me on a subconscious level from all the past lives and experiences I have had. I may decide to give myself permission to have a peek at those lives for reference in this one, to aid me on my journey. I do this through meditation, or by giving myself permission to soul journey in a meditational state; in my dreams, both day-dream and night-dream states; or just by accepting assistance from my guides or energy forces that work within my daily life, as these lessons and the experience gained from my past lives might aid me in a better understanding of the lessons I chose to learn in this lifetime.

Some might ask after reading this description, "What does it feel like?" Or, "What happens to you in this state of innerspace?"

For me, what happens is more felt inside my body. I have a peaceful knowledge that I am not ever alone. There is a collective consciousness of earned wisdom in soul state, "a presence you cannot usually see with your naked eye." It feels like a mass of collective, loving existence is supporting me in all my choices - without judgment and with acceptance in my process and the choices I make. What happens is that I gain wisdom; not the kind of wisdom I would gain in my brain from daily human education, but a wisdom that surpasses even logic. It is just a loving wisdom that radiates from my heart, from the inside of it to the outside of my body. I call this educational institution "Soul School" and I elaborate a bit more on this educational concept of learning as you read along with me and I share with you. I would very much like to take you on my journey, so let's start at my beginning, just because we all have one.

My Journey to Healing

The Beginning

What started out as an interesting observation to me is that I came to realize I have very few early childhood memories. In doing some research on this subject, I have come to understand it's a rather common occurrence. I can look at baby pictures - I have one in particular that my mother pulled out from the family archives. I am told by my mom that I am 18 months old. I am standing up in a car passenger seat with the most inquisitive eyes. I could see by the picture my poor mother was going to have her

hands completely full. I still have a bald head; she tells me it took a very long time for her little girl to have any hair. When I look at that picture, it stirs a familiar feeling in my heart and warms me, and lets me know by my pretty little dress and sweet disposition that I was cared for and loved. I am so drawn to this photo. It makes my soul smile when I look at the picture of the little girl; the effect is a powerful healing.

But it's simply not that simple. I came from a rather large family by today's standards, of five children, me being the first. My mom was a stay-at-home mom until we were all pretty well on our way to school, and then she worked, as well, to help support the growing needs of our family. My father worked hard to provide for our family and we moved a lot for the first few years. My parents were young, they were madly in love, and I honestly remember the stories of their meeting and whirlwind courtship. My parents share the story about their engagement. My parents, at the time, boarded in separate housing in London. My grandmother spent one day a week in London to get away. On those days, she would visit her daughter, my mom, who was going to school in London. She went to Wells Academy, which was a business school. One nice spring day in May, my parents walked my grandmother back to the train station. My father was so nervous about asking my mother to marry him that he carried her diamond ring ten blocks tucked under his armpit until they retuned back home. From my understanding, my father walked to my mother's residence, they walked downtown to meet my grandmother, walked her to the train station, and walked back to my mom's house. My dad then proceeded to get down on one knee professing his love, and the rest is 60 years of marriage and history!

I won't get into any details of the functions or dysfunction and the dynamics of our family, but I will say it gave me a significant amount of education to use to help myself grow up and out of some very light and dark places, each time climbing to another level of unconditional universal love, there for the taking and free for all of us. Our family grew quickly, my parents learning and growing up with their five children, all of us trying to figure life out. There are only eight years separating the oldest to the youngest of five children, so to say there were no lessons to be had is simply not the truth. I have fond memories of Christmas being so good. Every year there were extras: heartfelt gifts of love, some bought, some made by hand. I don't know how they managed it, but they did. I also remember birthdays being very special. Homemade, thought-out gifts and our favorite dinner and homemade cake. My parents took me shopping and purchased the most stunning dress for my grade eight graduation. It was coral and beautiful. Again, I am not sure how they managed all they did, but it happened.

I understand now that growing through the life experiences I did and, more importantly, making choices, actually brought me to this space in time where I have the ability to collectively sort out and also have the power to shed, both physically and on a soul level, what does not make me happy or at peace. I get to choose!

Choice in every moment can change your personal history. Power in your personal choice is the most important ingredient you have to find your peace.

My mother will attest that her child always needed answers: What? Why? Where? As long as I can recall I have always seemed to question direction and discipline. I can only imagine this causing frustration and, I am guessing, difficulty for my parents, teachers, guides, and friends, at times. I could be quite determined when I was being taught something that just did not register to be my truth, and most times, I would just do it my way and continue to beat my own drum. I like to say I feel like I have been educated my entire life in an educational institute I call "Soul School."

To further explain this theory, I feel we have two educational systems within and around us. As we are three-dimensional beings - Body, Ego Mind, and Spiritual - the easiest focus for humans and the one that can be simply explained is the physical space we occupy, the outer world to which we are connected. If I were to make a personal observation, I would guess that eighty-five percent of our population buys into the ways of the physical world. In other words, they best relate to the history and origin of their families, excel in the educational systems, and grow into and conform to what they believe to be their truth and life in physical presence, occupying the body in which they reside. This space is what I call the "safe zone."

I heard a very interesting comment recently from a friend who happens to be a physic medium. This comment resonated truth in my ego, as well as my soul. She stated that every person is unique, like each snowflake, and they all have their own thumbprint. "We are all important, and precious and rare. We all have something to offer to ourselves and the world we live in." She then said, "Most people just don't share this way." This hit me hard in my heart for many reasons. It made me have a deeper desire to connect and fall in love with people, to reach out and share my personal experience, and, in my bare open heart space, offer a place of healing or refuge.

The Agony of Loss

How do I continue to captivate you on a subject that is personal and something I hope you can claim and make personal for you? Of course, it is by telling you something personal. That is how we fall in love with each other and make a connection. We all have a personal story. We all have made choices. We all have suffered loss.

My first personal, devastating loss occurred when I was seventeen. He was a boy, my first love. You know the kind: the one you would follow into the sunset. He died tragically in a car accident. For years, I felt tremendous guilt around the accident as he was coming to visit me, and a horrible chain of events led him to a car crash. He lived on life support for three long days, and his parents were kind enough to allow me to sit with them and wait for the miracle that never happened to their baby and my sweetheart. I remember that I had had some kind of premonition about this accident, as I would often say to him, "If anything ever happens to you, please don't ever leave me until I can say goodbye to you." So, as it unfolded months later, he did wait for me to come to see him in Intensive Care, and although he could not talk to me, as I held his hand he did say goodbye to me. His respirator and heart rate increased as I stood by his bed as if to let me know he was with me, connected to me. Then he stopped breathing and the machines stopped beeping and he was gone. He just left me in body. That night as I lay in my bed thinking of him, I got very scared and felt all alone. Suddenly, I felt this rush of warm, fluid-like substance enter my being and envelope me in warm love. I know it was my love and I know he was saying, "I am here with you still in spirit." I fell asleep with this incredible peace inside of me, knowing that truth. However, the seventeen-year-old broken girl part of me died a physical ego death, and that death stayed with me, scarring me for thirty years. I carried him in my inner space and built a shrine for thirty years. I built a fortress of wire and blood around him in my inner space. He became unreachable, and so did the other relationships I developed around him. I was living in two worlds and had no idea on a conscious level.

Now, this is where my story has a twist and gets interesting. He saved me! His death saved me and built me into this being of love, light, and compassion. This heartache made me dig deep down inside and find a way to heal my inner space. His love for me saved me and encouraged me to finally find a way to love myself in my brokenness. He was so patient in my healing process as I know a piece of him stayed with me throughout all those years, silently guarding and protecting me until I grew enough to release him fully and free him entirely.

I made several poor choices in the aftermath of my physical tsunami. I met a man, married him, and had two very beautiful children. I was broken though, and my brokenness leaked out and was toxic to the insecurity and the hurt inside my inner space. I was not reachable, and, as a result, I made unhealthy choices.

I don't blame my former husband or my children for the dysfunction, as it had nothing to do with their existence. I did, however, make choices that haunted me for years, leaving me in a wake of pain and destruction to further secure my fortress in my inner space.

To say I was unhappy in those years is not entirely true. I was more lost and broken. That would be more accurate. As the marriage progressed and the unhealthy relationship continued, we found ourselves at a place of zero communication. We separated and moved on: he, with the children of our union; me, in a place of utter despair.

Again, this lesson of desperation gave me the gift of grace.

I, who had never taken drugs, drank alcohol, or smoked pot, ended up at 26 years old working at a bar, doing drugs, drinking and staying up all hours of the night. I would love to tell all the nitty gritty dirt in all of this timeframe of my life, but that is not the purpose of this book.

I lived with a very carefree, spirited woman who quickly taught me the tricks of the trade, took me under her wing, and coaxed me into survival mode. She was kind and I had never trusted kind, so instead of accepting her love, I looked for a motive. We had a disagreement as, in my sickness and broken heart, I misunderstood her kindness to mean something else entirely.

This lesson brought me to my knees and to an overdosing situation, which found me having a near-death experience. This is a painful memory, but at this time I want to elaborate and share my lesson of choice, action, and reaction.

I was working at that time in a bar in Port Elgin. It was a family business and was the hot spot at the time. We were busy. We had a full patio, restaurant, and evening entertainment. I worked some pretty long shifts and got pretty tired. I had some acquaintances at the time who supplied me with some pretty potent drugs to keep me going. I remember one particular night I had the night off. I was in the bar partaking in a few beverages, and a man asked me, "Do you want to go to my car and smoke some weed with me?" I agreed. I must have had a whole legion of angels with me because what followed was horrifying! I remember walking back into the bar and all the walls were tilted and the floor slanted. I remember going to the restroom and feeling like I was completely out of control. This was in January so there was snow and ice on the ground. It was extremely cold. It was still pretty early, maybe around 10:00 pm. All of a sudden, I was not feeling very well and after I came out of the restroom, the man I had been doing this with grabbed my arm, scaring me, demanding I go out and park in his vehicle with him. I believe he had other intentions for me. I was fortunate that another friend was paying attention to what was happening and he intervened. He quickly scooped me up, aided me to his car, and started to drive me home. I asked my friend to take me to the Southampton Hospital Emergency Department, which he did. On entering the Emergency Department, it was obvious to everyone that I was in an extreme state of drug and alcohol intoxication. I remember being put in a room. I remember lying on the bed with my boots and coat off. I was wearing a blue-jean dress and brown leotards. I remember the doctor coming in and evaluating me and telling the nurse he needed to "… go and get something so we can inject her." I was petrified. I remembered thinking, "He has no idea what I had ingested in my system." He was not aware, and I was unable to tell him, that the joint I had smoked had been laced with something, so how could he inject something in me to counteract the substance in my body? I had a full-fledged panic attack.

I ran out of the hospital and down a hill and laid in a small ditch by a pond that was near the hospital. I was lying on my back and I distinctly remember my life coming to end. It was so real that thirty-five years later, the memory is still crystal clear and so are the emotions. It was like my life essence started to leave my body, traveling up my legs and leaving my arms. It was a collective gathering in my chest. I lost feeling in the other parts of my body. I saw my life choices flashing in my mind like a movie I was watching myself in. At that moment, I felt a warm loving presence above me and a cold dark presence at my feet. I remember thinking, "If I choose to leave my body in this cold ditch tonight, I will be torn between this warm loving energy and this cold energy and be in this state for a very long time." I think that may have been hell for me; a place where I could never have closure or find peace; feeling love and warmth, but never able to have it; being held by the cold energy keeping me from getting there. I remember at the time ripping the cross I wore off my neck and fighting my way up the icy cold hill in my stocking feet. I remember walking to the nearest restaurant on the corner and walking through the front door. I remember not paying attention to the stares I was receiving from the people in the restaurant. I know my legs were bleeding and my hands were bleeding, and I can only imagine what I must have looked like. I walked to the back of the restaurant and there was a waitress taking an order on the phone. I took the receiver out of her hand without saying a word and gently hung the phone up. I then picked up the receiver until I heard the dial tone, handed it to her, and asked her to please call this number, my ex-husband's, and she did. At the same time that he arrived to get me, the police arrived at the restaurant. The doctor had put out a missing person distress call on my behalf. My ex-husband took care of the situation and drove me straight to the Owen Sound Mental Health Institution.

To say that experience was humbling is one of the biggest understatements of my life. It was pivotal to my existence and my inner space journey. I was alive in the weirdest, most broken, but yet whole way. I put on my mountain boots and started climbing and, most importantly, accepted the wiser hands, both physically and spiritually, that were being offered to me with wise love. I had so many deaths in that four-month sabbatical. I suffered death but was still living, breathing, existing, broken. I was learning to live without the extensions of my children and the life I had once had. It was like we had been amputated, but still had phantom pains. I know my children's pain was worse as they were far too young to even try to comprehend this loss. I had stopped running and fell face first into a wall of truth. I was facing things full on, and nothing was any more important than trying to start the long process of putting my life back in order.

The Cycle Continues....

Through that near-death on so many levels experience, I ended up in a hospital for a four-month sabbatical, fighting for my life, trying to decide if I wanted to reinvest in my life or make another choice. Let me elaborate here. I had a doctor say to me during my rehabilitation therapy - that is what they called one-on-one sessions back in the 1980's - "Tracey, you could go either way," meaning I could give up on life, existing in and out of institutions, being reintroduced to medication and new therapies, or I could reinvest in living and learn how to rebuild my life. Doctors of the mind, in those days, did not mince their words. Nor did they offer quick fix solutions. We all, in the 1980's, were able to voice our words, make solid plans, and communicate in a verbal context. Rock bottom, this was the very first time I realized how sick, how sad, and how alone I really was. I had lost everything important to me: my family, my beautiful children. I was so crushed and so lost. It was the first time I felt my inner space and connected with the spiritual essence I was born with. It was my first genuine encounter with the God-source that is our birthright, and it was the first time I was broken enough to hear my options.

To say that I felt amputated from my babies and totally depressed would probably be an understatement. I am not quite sure still to this day how a seven-year-old boy whose mother handed him a box of Smarties on the staircase of his home, saying to him "Mommy has to leave now," ever got over the fear and the pain of losing his lifeline. How a five-year-old, beautiful girl ever emotionally survived the scar tissue on her heart. I was there one day, gone the next. There are many unpleasant things I could say about how their father dealt with and decided all our fate. He made decisions and choices, wielding his power, hand, and cards, and I folded, letting him decide for all of us. To say we all have not suffered over the choices would be a lie. We have all been striving to survive and grow towards becoming decent human beings. The price tag is still a numbing effect, like being frozen at the dentist. We have all experienced repercussions due to the choices we made. We have all come out the other side of our choices; these choices set our destiny. When you make hard choices, or personal sacrifices, you seem to have a different kind of understanding about life. I left our home and returned to my parents' home, and the slow process of rebuilding continued for me there. My children's fate was decided by my ex-husband, and they resided with him and his new partner.

Still in this state of limbo, in a new town separated from the life I had and still wondering what to do, where to start, what to build in my innerspace, miracles started happening. Places and things were given to me, both from this physical world, but also from a spiritual place when my old perceptional actions and habits acted on auto pilot, when I felt I was running out of options. How many of us, myself guilty of this, when we feel trapped or are in trouble, cry out for our God to save us, to make things right, to take away our pain or troubles? This was the beginning of my understanding that the great "I Am" or God-source is just as much a part of my existence as my DNA, and we are one team, united. We are all entwined in a universal energy that connects us, making us one unit. I really understood that we were a team and not a separation, but a single, functioning unit.

It was a spark of recognition that I belonged to a universal, real team. It was my initiation to my first grade of Soul School. Like worldly education, I excelled in some subjects and had to repeat others. The lessons and actions of virtue, for instance, I get stuck on and repeat time and time again. It requires great energy and great concentration, understanding that patience is the action that requires the attribute itself. I have a quicker recognition of when I need to be kinder and loving, all due to imprinting and putting lessons learned into practice.

The next few years, I was in and out of what I call "survival mode." I was making choices that were more impulsive than healthy. I was still broken and instead of picking choices for a healthy self, I was picking choices for a broken self. It's been my experience that when you do that, it takes the pressure off you to change and gives you a reason to put your time and energy into helping fix other broken people. You attract what you are and what you think about. I kept attracting the sameness in others for partners and friends. These actions seemed to be stunting my growth. I remained in this stagnant space for several years. So, I guess you could say I repeated a few primary grades in Soul School. Not fun, but if you don't learn the lesson of love the first time, it seems to me the gentle, unconditional love of the great source most of us call God keeps sending you a new fishing line with another scenario attached. He gives us so many new chances to learn how to be the best person we can be. That excites me so much! It's like we get a new chance every single time we realize we could have made a kinder, more loving choice in every single moment of the day. Who says we cannot all be billionaires? Who says being rich is just about money? The soul world does not exchange currency!

I found a new love. He was broken too. That brokenness attracted me to a familiar space. It was a fast three days later and we had made a choice. I won't get into the details of the next seventeen years, but we both grew and we supported what we could and to this day remain friends. He taught me many things, so I would like to share with you, and I have his permission to do so.

My spiritual gifts were manifesting faster than I could even understand. One of the biggest gifts to this day was reuniting with my children on a consistent, structured visiting schedule. He gave me back my children. He was as committed to them as he was to me. He also had two little girls and I did, as well, fall in love with them. We were all trying to be normal, live normal, in broken places. Yes, it was a recipe for disaster! It was destined to sink like the Titanic. Yes, we were just as naïve as the people on that invincible ship. We thought we had it all. We thought we were invincible! But we married initially for the wrong reasons. We both agree that we actually used each other. He thought I could save him from the broken heart of his first marriage. I thought he could give me back my broken children. We used that against each other until we fell out of love and just existed in a broken state of marriage. We were never best friends. We only understood a brokenness that was never addressed and only grew into a toxic, redundant relationship.

For a few years, we just coasted and tried to raise the children. We were simply trying to do the best we could, for them and for us. We worked hard to blend the family and survive in our own broken space. When you have issues you have never addressed, or even admitted, you cannot make changes. It's really that simple. I found we danced around subjects that were touchy and subjects we did not want to claim or be responsible for. In laymen's terms, we were growing differently. He escaped to the silent world of television and a small trailer, and I turned to a religious charismatic group at my church. We continued this slow dance until we danced right into a separation.

There are some times in our lives when universal energy seems to send cement bricks our way in a hail storm effect! Thank God we have bullet-proof umbrellas to soften the blows. This bold acclamation helps me realize that the seventeen years I shared with my second husband taught us that although we struggled with the reality of the dysfunction, we were still able to accept each other in our separated relationship, giving us each the space we needed to grow independently. Knowing the difference in a state of comfort versus a state of restlessness is the gift that we have both received and continue, as friends, to talk about to this day. We are so lucky to be good people, with hearts big enough to risk another broken relationship so that we can grow into what the universe around both of us has called us to.

Love saved us! Love taught us both what we needed to find in all essence to lead us to wholeness, so we could take all our broken pieces and put us back together.

Sometimes, I hear a quote or some wisdom in a quote that brings me back to my inner space and, in one heartbeat, makes sense or resonates on a frequency that is instant, like this one I have written in my workspace: "How did you know you were meant to be a healer? I kept falling in love with broken people. Then, why are you alone? Because I am broken too! So, I am falling in love with myself to get a taste of my own medicine."

Transformation

About thirteen years into my second marriage, I had an opportunity to sing, all because I was sitting on a chopped down tree stump and heard a very distant, crisp voice say behind my back, "You're going to sing for me now." I got that shiver. You know the one you get when you are in this kind of a moment. The one you cannot explain logically. That shiver, the one that starts from the inside of you. I responded in the cheekiest way and said, "Really? And just how are you going to make all this happen? I don't sing Christian music." But the voice kindly said, "One door will open at a time." And so it went.

Within two years, I was lead to a minster who, after he listened to my testimonial, handed me over four original masterpieces of his own cherished arrangements. He was kind and he was aware of what true "inner soul" meant when he lovingly allowed his thought and love for his God to be recorded by a stranger professing that a voice spoke to her and directed her to sing for him. I had the best recording mind and gifted friend, with the same kind of drive, love, and passion for music (his language of choice), guide me and work with me for hours. The music was my first step into claiming my inner space, letting go, and trusting something that happened by first choosing, and then deciding to follow through on the choice. Yes, it was by my action, but the reaction to my action was mixed with divine anointing. I will try to explain this.

When you choose and you say yes, you are aided by a universal energy that makes things happen. Some people call this the power of attraction. This recording was the result of the power of attraction suggested by a divine energy. It matters not that the music then was spread to the masses or the effect it had on the person who was anointed by it, or even that it was blessed by the Vatican in Rome by Pope John Paul II, as well as people expressing that the power of this music changed them, moved them, and helped them. What I am trying to say is what happens after your action is not your personal business. It becomes the personal business of the person experiencing the effect of your loving action. The act itself pays it forward, without looking for the rewards that may or may not come. Be rewarded in the simple act of your action. Personal validation is the key here. Feel the peace in your action, not in the reaction that may or may not come back to you.

SECRETARIAT OF STATE

FIRST SECTION · GENERAL AFFAIRS

From the Vatican, 5 March 2002

Dear Miss Joosten,

The Holy Father was pleased to receive the copy of your CD, and he has asked me to thank you. In accordance with your request, I am now returning the second copy to you.

His Holiness will remember you in his prayers, and he invokes God's abundant blessings upon you.

Sincerely yours,

Monsignor Pedro López Quintana
Assessor

Miss Tracey Joosten
100 Bradley Street
Strathroy, ON
N7B 3Y9

I guess you could say I am a bit of a rebel and a one-man island. I never think anything is impossible. I just feel it, then do it or hear it, say it or love it, and then choose to like it. I try to live daily from my inner space. So, there are times when my massive gray area of living and functioning ruffles black and white logic. I also have a real personal issue with boundaries. Those who know me may smile at this comment, but truly, this has been a huge struggle for me my entire life. I have painstakingly repeated the eighth grade of Soul School for eons! It is the grade where you are given information on boundaries. I still struggle with them. I still have a hard time distinguishing between polite conversation and an invitation or invasion on a person's journey!

I have had many loving hands and hearts involved and supporting me while singing through this period of my life: a supportive partner who accepted the time it took and was devoted to the quest; strong, amazing friends with arms out, quietly in the background helping with the CD release party. One particular gentle friend laid out all the food and helped make it beautiful. The efforts and the masses of combined love created a lasting memory, a treasure I call "divine gems." They have their own heart space in my soul's inner space.

I recall a time when I started singing differently. I was an open vessel of divine love and purpose. I remember letting my body be used as a powerful tool so that God and his holy spirits of angels could use me to touch the masses and reach them in song. I remember one particular song I recorded called "Abba Father" that was a song we sang in our prayer group as a combined spirit, in unison, singing praise to God. I wanted that particular song to be recorded on the CD to dedicate to the prayer group. The CD was called "Traces of the Heart" - appropriate for the project to which I felt a divine calling. I remember the day it was recorded. It was in my producer's basement. He had all the equipment set up and I was in my stocking feet, wearing a t-shirt and blue jeans. The song was recorded in one take, and musicians know that it is impossible to sing a song and not have to re-record it a few times. In all honesty, my diaphragm filled up as if it had a mind of its very own. The breath control was amazing and divine; the pitch perfect, rich, full of hundreds of souls in song channeled through my body. I know this song on the CD has healed many wounded people.

Testimonials are soul food. One particular lady showed up at the release party. She stood right up in the congregation and told her story. It was a jaw-dropper and as she spoke and told her part in the music's journey, it was incredible to hear. I would like to share her experience.

This beautiful person stated that she was walking through the park two years prior and she heard a voice singing from a nearby pavilion. She did not know it was me and she did not even know the context of the song I was singing. The song was "House of the Rising Sun" by the Animals. She remembers it because my voice touched her deeply enough to say, "God, she should be singing for you." And from that day on she prayed it would happen. Two years later, she was standing at a photocopier at a local convenience store making copies for Sunday School and she happened to see a flyer of my CD release party, indicating the time and location. She stopped what she was doing and showed up at the church and came in to tell her story. I don't believe in coincidence - only perfect, divine timing!

It has been my experience that once Pandora's Box has been opened, you don't fit the same if you try to go back. Parts of you stick out of the box in

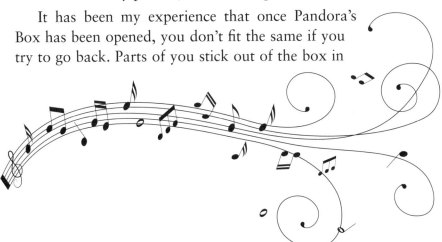

which you once felt safe or complacent. Trust me when I say complacent. It is usually a warm sticky bun, yummy kind of feeling existing in a place of routine and comfort. It tastes good to eat your familiar, favorite kinds of food. It feels safe wearing the same comfortable clothing and having a sense of security that comes from existing in routine. The problem for me is it's boring and I get restless. In the past when I was not making such healthy choices, it was easy to fall back into routine. Whether it was the best thing for me or not, it was comfortable. In saying this, I realized after my second husband handed me a very beautiful anniversary card that, although he truly meant the words, he did not mean them for me.

Still married to the second man and still in this dysfunctional space trying to make our relationship work, I made a huge decision after considerable reflection. I decided to set up a test and acted on some of the words in the card. Not the response I expected! Or maybe it was. I realized that my second husband never dreamed about our future. He just existed, and I thought how sad that was. I really considered his life, maybe for the first time, and I thought he would choose to never change his unhappiness. I decided then that it was up to me to choose it for us. That started a five-month painful process of separation and another seven months of closure.

Everyone thought I was out of my mind. And in all reality, it was my inner space and soul world dominating my ego world. I remember the evening before I left my second marriage. My Reiki Master took me to a healing drumming workshop. I was the person volunteered to be the vessel of healing. That night, the universe provided another window, another opportunity for healthy choice, and so it happened.

I would like to share something now that made it extremely difficult to even consider a separation at that time. My former husband and I had taken on the responsibility of two teenage girls who had just lost their mother to a very long, serious illness. We, their mother and I, were given to each other and we chose to take care of each other over a two-year period of time. The children asked my former husband and me, and he and I made a promise to all of them, that if she were to leave us, we would make arrangements and have the girls live with us. It was a difficult transition for all of us. The girls and their mother belonged to a church that had different faith and beliefs than we did, so to say this was easy would be incorrect. It most certainly was not easy for all of us involved in the decision. In the end, they did come to reside with us. They were still living at our home when I decided to leave the marriage. I did find an apartment with two bedrooms and fully intended to take the youngest one, who at that time was turning fifteen. The oldest girl was off to school several miles away. She was intending to come home on weekends. I invited them along to go look for an apartment. We chose one and, in the end, they both chose to stay with my second husband in our matrimonial home. It was a very bad time for those girls, but looking back, he needed them more and they also needed a male figure in their lives. To this day, they remain family. I feel so blessed that he is such a great person who loves so much from his heart. He has given those girls exactly the stability they needed and they continue to be blended family.

A few months later, my estranged husband asked for help finding a piece of jewelry he was distraught over losing. I went over and helped him recover it, as I had a clear vision of its location. He was ashen when we moved the big wardrobe and it was under a pile of dirt. We had the most honest discussion of our seventeen years after finding his ring. He took my hands and said, "You're different. It will be easy for me to find another person as I am in the eighty-fifth percentage of the normal populous. You, Tracey - it will take you some time, if ever, to find someone who is strong enough to be with you." He did find his love shortly after and he is so completely smitten. I am honestly happy he found his soul mate. He deserves to be happy. We all do. He also said something to me that is tattooed on my inner space heart. He said, "Your courage and your strength have set us free and we can now have happiness in our lives." That still carries me through on rainy days. When you rise above yourself and take a peek at your surroundings, it's a clearer view and a whole different perspective. It is far easier said than done! After all, we are indeed human.

Moving on can have you stubbing a few toes and ruffling more than a few feathers. People stake a claim in you when you emotionally invest in them. It's like you become emotionally a part of their world as they know it and you buy into the relationships. Yes, it's a choice, but most times it's more complicated depending on the amount of "you" that has been invested in the relationship.

Learning to Understand

Gifts of the Spirit

At this point in my life, I had a few levels of Reiki under my belt. If I may share some of my education with you, I would like to elaborate on just how I fell in love with the practice.

While in a group of like-minded spirits around the time of the whole "hearing God speak to me on a personal level" thing, I asked for some gifts of the spirit. I asked specifically for the gift of love. I asked specifically for the gift of wisdom and was granted these with all the fruits that come with the gifts. You know people often say, "Be careful what you wish for." I caution you to be mindful, always, of what it is you desire, as there is always a price tag for and repercussions from what you honestly and truly desire.

My life started to change and manifest quickly. I was led to meditation to try and quiet the giant growing in me that I was having a hard time containing in my inner space, and that led me to a seven-day meditation retreat in Pennsylvania. It was excruciating! I know for a fact, I shed several lives and suffered a few physical ego deaths at this retreat, again hearing a calming voice instructing me to curl up in a fetal position and let it run its course. It was incredible! The experience was like going into labour in a soul connection instead of a physical birth. It changed me, and humbled me, and encouraged me to continue. We sat in meditational prayer several times a day, in twenty-minute meditational prayer sessions. I was not sure I ever got to the place

I was supposed to get to, but then, what place is that? That was the lesson for me. Any place intended to be good is the perfect place. Because we could not speak, we worked using our cognizance instead of our regular physical senses.

Another woman attending the retreat was particularly beautiful! I was drawn to her. She glowed like the sun, and just being around her made me feel grace and peace without any verbal communication. She was an angel. I was informed later on in the week that she was a practicing Reiki Master. I had, until then, never heard the word. So, after the seminar I went to a book store, bought my first book on the chakra system, and was absorbed in what the soul world meant through this kind of healing energy. What I had come to understand at the time was that Reiki is a form of hands-on healing. It is a technique you are attuned to in forms of degrees by a Reiki Master. It is an awakening of Consciousness. I was given the first two degrees of my practice as gifts from beautiful friends who believed it would help others if I were to become a practitioner.

My Reiki Master was a God-send and, at the time, I was unaware that I had been given the gift of the perfect Master for me as I had no idea where this practice, this lifestyle that was so rich and divine, was going to take me. I was gifted with my degrees by a wise sage, who taught me slowly, one on one, at her home. I understand that now, you can learn all your degrees in one weekend of in-class instruction and some people choose this method. For me, I had to learn one degree at a time, and digest and practice this gift for many years before I finally decided, through much contemplation, to become a Reiki Master Teacher.

To be honest, the main reason I held back from attaining this level was the fear of being responsible for passing Reiki on to others. This may seem silly in retrospect, considering all the courage I seem to have in my words and all the tough choices so far in my life that seemed harder than this one. I was thinking deep down that I love and cherish this way of channeling and healing so much and have witnessed hundreds of miracles. How was I to determine if someone needed to learn Reiki? My answer was simple and direct. This was not about me or the way I might feel about teaching a client. This was about the journey they chose. It is not my business to ever judge or determine or claim anything from anyone. That is about ego and power. Rather, it is always about someone coming to me and asking for what they need. I just get to be the person asked to be hands for the source of the healing they are seeking or the wisdom for which they need direction.

Humbled, and with a fresh perspective on this new insight, I took my final and last Master Degree. It was perfect, as all of the degrees were, and many healing tears were shed between my Master and myself who, together, have had so many deep-as-canyons healings and sharings. I will mention two things here, between her and me, and I have her permission to do so.

One day, she came to hear me sing at a Relay for Life gathering. I had just lost a dear friend to cancer two days prior. I sang for her, her daughters, the crowd, the people gathered there. My beautiful Mentor and Master's face was in the crowd, giving me strength she did not even know she was giving me. After the song, she found me and said the most profound thing to me. She said, "I used to believe and think you were mine, but after today, I know you belong to everyone." We just hugged and shared this moment of something bigger than both of us, happening in the masses of broken people all affected by cancer. We knew a bigger space in our hearts had opened. It was a moment that was bittersweet, filled with love and emotions and feelings. It was honest and kind and loving and real.

Another amazing memory for me is this, and, as I have stated, we had and still have so many it's hard to choose; however, this one is quite profound.

After my teacher training, we were discussing our history together. When I first started meditating with my Reiki teacher soon after meeting each other, I brought Jesus with me. She brought our Reiki Master, Dr. Mikao Usui. These were the two Ascended Masters with whom we were working at the time we first connected. When meditating together at the end of a session around the time of my last degree, she experienced a vision of Jesus and me with Mikao. When we shared a moment in conversation after our session, we knew we had come together in full circle and we both realized we are all part of one collective energy, being one in the same but keeping our own individual identity, meditating and joining collectively as one in spirit.

I want to share another very personal experience that is sacred to me. I might be stepping outside my special keepsake box, but I think you are all worth it. Please bear with me as I try to paint this picture of my experience in my final attunement.

My Master had completed the attunement and sat in a chair across from me in silence, allowing me the space and time to fully appreciate my experience. I found my spirit form leaving me and walking on a celestial road. I could see the stars under my feet, and the road was like clear coat. I was walking towards a huge being of light. I can only tell you, I had a sense it was God - the God I have come to know inside me. To my left, I could see figures but no faces. They were all in a line and all different sizes and shapes. I honestly thought to myself at the time that some of these shapes were not the humans I was familiar with, but I knew they were teachers, scholars, and doctors of the soul. I met up with the God-source and can only describe it as heart-stopping awe. The source had no face, just a huge presence that was too bright to look at directly, so I lowered my head and the source handed me an orange, non-material scroll. It had no substance, but it was substance all the same, with a message from God: "Congratulations, Tracey! You have graduated and can now step in place in the line."

I was so overwhelmed in that moment! I had only one true thought as He placed me in the line to the left where there was an empty space that fit me, molded me, and tucked me in, conforming to the mass. "I am home, and we are united in a collective energy of love."

The Amazing Power of Love, Kindness, Forgiveness

Once open to your innerspace, it is very difficult to find someone who sees past all the differences that are more from the soul world than this world. I had no intention of falling in love with my soulmate, best friend, and life partner. It happened and the result has been my best growing years ever. He has become the other half of my functioning heart. Both physically and spiritually, Joe has become my best friend. One of the earliest comments he said out loud to me was, "There is something different about you." The fact that he said that is still the glue keeping us connected and accountable to and for each other. He guides me and suggests things to me that cause me to think outside the box. He believes in me in ways that continue to help aid my growth and my mission. If I were to have a mission statement, it would simply be to love one heart at a time. That is what I really try to be accountable for, to strive for.

I always call myself a "gazillionaire" and I know I challenge my partner daily by my way of living my life. It's not that I am not responsible or even lack accountability; it's just that I don't care about or get hung up on worldly wealth. He has another survival outlook when it comes to providing for his family. I know something richer in my innerspace. It's like I have a secret, and the secret is peace of mind and a faith that sees me through on a different plane. It's like I live between two worlds and the interconnect brings me a satisfied result of fullness. It is not a cop-out at all that I choose to live this way. It is my choice. It is an earned wisdom that I know I will always learn and grow and find a positive awakening, even in my painful lessons. My life partner, who makes me a better person daily, believes in me. In some ways, he is my biggest fan. He supports me, listens to me, and watches what happens when people ask me for a "service" or help. He has witnessed things he does not understand, but his soul knows it is for the good of the person. He has the ability to empower us both to be a cohesive unit and still be secure as independents. He is the reason I am writing this book and he actually titled it. Yes, he was the one who first suggested it. It had never, ever crossed my mind. He feels the world needs ordinary people doing extraordinary acts of kindness. He is one of the kindest, most gifted beings I have ever had the privilege of loving. He keeps me humbled, grounded, and human. He makes me belly laugh and reminds me, when I start to get too deep or analyze too much, to stop and just breathe. He teases me saying, "Tracey, you are taking all the oxygen out of the room! Please stop and breathe with me!"

Being kind and being honestly accountable are your two primary, most important tools in the process of living in your innerspace.

Being kind is a free investment, and I encourage you to use this gift and the energy it creates in every single action you either think or act on. Practice it! Use it when you know you are uncomfortable with the actual action of your kindness, and with your voice and body language. Watch the act work a miracle right before your eyes.

We are all human. We frequently invest emotionally in passionate confrontation, which we feel totally entitled to do. The dynamics of human nature and the way people choose to be are immensely fascinating. They can captivate me for many hours. And who am I to say or not say what and how people choose to conduct themselves while learning their own lessons? This manner of thinking has freed me from many a gut-wrenching, debilitating loss. All the things for which I thought I needed to be accountable or responsible were simply not the truth. That realization, to me, was a huge moment of growth. If I choose to be a part of a relationship or conversation I am invited into, I can choose to not take part in it and not hold myself accountable for any of what I thought was obligation or duty.

This realization was huge! And how did I get here? I got here by being completely truthful in my innerspace; hearing my soul, taking that truth, flooding it with kindness before sharing the wisdom that moment provides me. Taking that moment to catch my breath before responding with love and kindness! Love is the only answer for true peace!

This, you have heard so many times before, but it is the whole truth and nothing but the truth. That realization – that moment of enlightenment – came to me on the piggyback of Forgiveness.

To begin with, and some of you may find this awkward - and even backwards, I started by forgiving myself: Forgiving myself for leaving my family and my children that resulted in years of self-abuse and therapy; forgiving myself for abandoning my children, not so easy to attain. This does not mean you do not still suffer the consequences of your choices. What it does mean is that you experience a healing. You forgive and free yourself from the excruciating flogging you have repeated over and over again. The scar tissue remains to remind you that you have learned the lesson, but now you are able to look at yourself with kindness.

Then, I forgave myself for not buying into my relationships and picking easy outs. If I was not invested completely and emotionally, how could I be all in or committed to this chosen way of living? They all, up until my current partner, had a hidden agenda and self-preservation motives, as did I. I could not be completely devastated or obliterated in a safe zone, so my heart was never fully committed, leaving holes in my innerspace world.

Two things happen when you find the whole partner you have been seeking and with whom you have been blessed. You make someone else number one in a soul connection, and also, you become more vulnerable than you ever imagined you could ever be. These are gifts to help you grow and continue to change. It's rewarding and frightening, exciting and ever-changing. It is like the universal innerspace around you - the vastness - changes and recommits in every second of the day.

Being in a healthy space has given me wings and tools and reason to get up on those mornings when I feel warm and content to stay in the same position I was in in my mother's womb before birth. It's soft and warm and loving and safe under the covers of your warm, safe bed. It's heaven and it's a sabbatical we return to every time we sleep, just before we are fully conscious. It's peace and grace in its highest form and freedom from the constant demands and mandate of our waking world. It's addictive and we crave that memory on a subconscious level all the moments we are consciously going through during our day.

Love is really and truly all there is. Even better, we are all called to it. It's a natural progression and it's a choice. This is the thing and it really does get my ego off the hook: We are not called to like. Hence, all the difference for me in the world is the knowledge that I get to choose what I like or don't like. I get to buy all in or cash in my chips at any time I feel I am not being treated or respected in a way I feel deserving. And guess what, my friends? We all get to play on this same team. If something is offensive to anyone, that is really not my issue; it belongs to them and it is part of their innerspace journey to find their own amazing, personal answers in the journey of their own lessons. I often say these days, "Not my circus, not my monkey," but the same phrase applies, as well, when I stake a claim and say, "This is my circus; it is my monkey." The best part is we get to choose and we become personally accountable.

I am still a work in progress. I will be a work in progress until my last breath, as will you be. All we can do is buy into something that makes us feel something. Feeling something is living; feeling nothing is just simply existing!

We have and always will have a choice. The choice is neither good nor bad because, guess what? If we choose another angle during the lesson at hand, if we don't like the results, we get to try again. It's all truly that simple. I've heard it said, "There are no mistakes; there are only choices."

This reminds me of a time when I ate crème brûlée for lunch, in Las Vegas in the Paris Casino restaurant. It was sinfully delicious!

I made no excuses and had it for appetizer, main course, and dessert. I think I ate five in total over about an hour and a half span of time. I did suffer the consequences much later as a result of the choice I made that day. All choices have consequences. Some are worth the consequences. Some are valuable aids and tools along the way. Some choices are strictly for pleasure. In all choices, personal accountability is key!

I am lucky and I am blessed. It is my practice to tell people their good qualities. It has become a habit for me to try to rise above the negative, but in all honesty, I am still human, and I do say things that are hurtful and sometimes constitute a personal attack. In those times, if I dig deep, I am more quickly aware that I may need to be truly sorry, maybe even more accountable. It was my choice to grow to a place where I believe we all have a choice and we all have a responsibility to be personally accountable. Getting to this place has been immensely rewarding and freeing for me personally, resulting in great joy and peace in my life. It is my goal to share this joy and help others to achieve this level of peace and contentment in their lives. The only way I can achieve this goal is to be kind to one heart at a time. It is the only control I have, and it is the key to my peace in the only moment I have. If we learn to commit to paying love forward and not expecting anything in return, maybe, just maybe, hearts will catch on fire and ignite the world around us. And the masses will find freedom in the peace provided by these loving actions.

Soul School

I wanted to give you some of my personal history for two reasons. First, if you are still reading, you are interested in finding peace and the tools to help you attain it. And second, everyone can tap into their innerspace at a higher level of love in transition through choices and lessons.

When I mentioned Soul School, I literally meant that we go to Soul School. We learn our lessons through an intangible system of psychic and spiritual wisdom that comes to us through innate intelligence. I will pair them so readers who have not heard of them and their functions have a better understanding and can compare the functions. I needed to elaborate on some of the pain and the process that lead me here to this space. It has been extremely painful reopening the wounds and shedding some information on my process and choices, choosing specifically the lessons of humility and love. It has been interesting, sidestepping all the broken glass.

This process has stirred up memories I am not proud to talk about; it has caused me some pain, and even a few weeks of depression, the kind of depression you are not proud of and truly want to bury for all time. These memories can only bring to the surface what one thought had been healed and taken care of, only to remind you of the truth and the humility it takes to forgive yourself once more, and to forge on with a new flame of desire and love to help ignite someone else on their own journey of self-discovery. I really and truly understand that we are all worth a second, third, and even fourth chance to be redeemed and healed within our own personal innerspace.

I have listed below some tools of the soul trade, so to speak. These tools have been invaluable to me personally and they are truly authentic. I use these tools regularly to check in on myself and to help others find the ones they may start with or have been already using for years. I am so grateful for all the assistance and information we gather and receive on the spiritual side of our beings.

Vision/Clairvoyance (clear inner vision)

A clairvoyant receives extra sensory impressions and symbols in the form of "inner sight" or mental images which are perceived without the aid of the physical eyes, and beyond the limitations of ordinary time and space.

Hearing/Clairaudience (clear audio/hearing)

To perceive sounds or words and extra sensory noise from sources broadcast from spiritual or ethereal realm, in the form of "inner ear" or mental tones that are perceived without the aid of physical ear and beyond the limitations of ordinary time or space.

Feeling/Clairsentience (clear sensation or feeling)

To perceive information by a feeling within the whole body, without any outer stimuli related to the feeling or information.

Smelling/Clairscent (clear smelling)

To smell fragrance/odor, substance, or food which is not in one's surroundings.

Touch/Clairtangency
(clear touching – more commonly known as psychometry)

To handle an object or touch an area and perceive through the palms of one's hands information about the article or its owner or history that was not previously known by the clairtangent.

Taste/Clairgustance (clear tasting)

To taste a substance without putting anything in one's mouth.

Emotion/Clairempathy (clear emotion)

An empath is a person who can physically tune in to the emotional experience of a person, place, or animal.

For those who are not familiar with these methods, it is important to note that we all are provided with these tools and have the means to use and explore them by investing time and energy into the gifts that may work best for us.

I use a few more of these senses and am the most comfortable with two in particular:

> Clairvoyance - vision
>
> Clairsentience - feeling

When I started to practice over a decade ago, I was using Reiki and meditation. I have always practiced hands-on in my sessions, placing my hands directly on the chakras. These are energy wheels in your body that are specifically placed and colour coded. They are our soul's beautiful energy that lives in our human-formed bodies.

As I grew into my passion, always working, sensing, and seeing the ever-changing healing and capabilities each client brought with them, it never ceased to fascinate me that the healer within the client was forever present, and the client received the level of healing from within their own personal space. They were the healer of their own divinely-agreed healing on a self-conscious level. We still get to choose what we want healed. *One fascinating fact: I get to be the facilitator, and I, too, receive a healing!*

The truth is a very difficult thing to understand and, sometimes for me, even harder to accept. It is painful and not always pleasant. It has taken me a lot of years to try and live in my truth, as it takes time and energy to even discern my honesty. If you want the truth and you are seeking the truth, there is a certain fear we all go into that I believe is key to changing and loving your inner space.

I would like to share a conversation I have had with a client who was having a hard time sleeping as a result of a particular action.

Tracey: Good morning. Did you have a better sleep last night?

Client: I slept a bit better I guess

Tracey: Good! That is progress. I just know you are looking for a different way of learning this lesson and that belongs to you. It's not my business what you choose. I am just glad you are open to finding another, kinder way to deal with your part in the whole situation. You may choose to share what you have chosen to do with it or you may not. The truth is, at the end of the day, you and only you have to live with your choices.

Client: If I choose to do it this way, should I ask her boss if it's okay to talk to her while she is working?

Tracey: No. You are not seeking approval. You are seeking closure. She may share with her boss or she may not. She may be touched deeply and choose to keep it sacred.

Client: I just don't want to get into trouble.

Tracey: This is your lesson. Drop the fear factor. Be wise, strong, and loving. There is no self-protection by living an honest life. We just grow tougher skin and we have to pull up our big girl pants. The results of your actions are not about you. The action is your lesson. We cannot control the reaction after the action, nor waste our time and our energy trying to keep ourselves in a safe place after the exposure of our action.

Client: Ok.

Tracey: Life is better lived in wholeness when you are honestly living it, instead of trying to hide in your complacency from the masses of the world. That is called conforming and existing. There is boredom in existing. There is new life in living. Keep in mind, every choice comes with a price tag.

Client: When can I get a refund?

Tracey: When you are at the pearly gates in negotiation with a good-looking angel! (My attempt at humour!)

Client: I have been thinking, when I am asked why I chose to do what I did to her, I am going to respond, "I didn't do this to you; I did this to myself by speaking my truth, and in doing so I hurt you in the process." I am just trying to think about how she will react.

Tracey: You are becoming a professional. I will be paying you $200.00. You know in your heart you are honestly spending too much time on her reaction. You need to stop spinning your hamster wheel in your head and let it go. Move on.

Client: I know.

Tracey: You are just trying to keep your world safe, your ego safe, your heart safe.

Client: Yep.

Tracey: That is what people may not understand. You act or not; you live or exist. Existing is safe and stagnant and can cause health issues, depression, weight gain, and loneliness. Living in love actually stops regression, all those symptoms. You become young, vibrant, and alive through the act of living. However, there is a price tag for this choice and for every choice you make, negative or positive. There is always a price tag.

Client: And how do you live in love?

Tracey: When you live in love and become honest, you may tend to ruffle the feathers of the safe zone and the masses I call the eighty-five percenters. You live a lonelier life, and people who are not like-minded may choose to not be around you because you make them think. They then may choose to go back to their safe, familiar habits, even if they are not the healthiest choices. In choosing truth, they can become raw and exposed and too vulnerable. I just choose love first every time, without the thought of keeping myself safe.

Truth

Who I am may actually make a difference to a few small groups of people in my inner circle. I am just one small person trying to make a huge difference, trying to let people know that choice and truth are your most powerful assets. Truth is the first ingredient to happiness. Such a simplistic formula, yet easier said or thought about than actually acted on. It may take time to really understand what it is that will make you happy and then knowing it to be your truth. This takes a few methods.

The first course of action is to find out what your truth is. This may mean you have to sit in silence, go for a walk, or just be. This can be difficult for people, as most people are uncomfortable with silence. The beating of their own heart, the movements of the innerspace soul place that is so unfamiliar to the voices, and the power of the ego world can be unsettling. But in your silence, you will hear a small whisper of your truth, wants, needs; the desires that are yours alone, but have been suppressed by the pressures, wants, needs and mandates of the world around you. The God and the loving energy I have come to know as one inside of me wants this for all of us. As we experience the God within, so does our Creator. I truly believe this to be true.

The next step is to be brave and allow your truth to seep into you on all levels. Know it. Feel it. Claim it. Re-act...notice how I say "re-act" and not "act." RECOGNITION of your truth will manifest your happiness much quicker, saving valuable time.

I have worked on this belief over the past year, and it has manifested in ways I am still reeling over. Let me try to explain.

In spending valuable time on myself to try to become a better, healthier, well-rounded person, I came to understand that I used to try to "fix" others around me. I came to realize I was offering my complete heart and soul to a person. In this realization - not that it was "bad" or "good" - I came to understand that if I spent time and energy on others who had a need for something I could offer them, "the action" made me feel validated and powerful.

In the end, it was very apparent that although it was feeding my ego, these relationships were actually stunting my growth and not feeding the needs of my own soul. I did not even realize I was not being truthful to my own growth and needs. This was an interesting lesson for me. These actions designed to help others were almost a form of addiction that made me feel very good about myself. I had very good intentions, but, in my truth, these intentions were sometimes more for me than for the person I was trying to help. I am now working very hard on offering the gifts I have been given to people who might be able to use them to aid their own personal journey, establishing "healthy boundaries" in the process.

Last year (2015) was one of the most painful years in quite some time. In my truth that was bubbling just beyond the surface of my smiling demeanor, I suffered great personal loss and heartache, including some very close relationships: some family, some soul friendships.

In my personal truth, after validation and reflection, I had to cut some individuals off as we were simply growing differently. I always say I am called to love everyone and that will never ever change. I simply had more lessons to learn and could not learn them from forces that did not allow me the freedom or space I required for the personal growth that was happening inside my spiritual body. In my truth, it was too hard to fight the differences and it was stunting my personal growth and lessons. I believe the situation was stunting their growth, as well.

I try very hard not to be a negative force, but to focus truly on the powerful effect that unconditional love may have on people and my actions towards them.

In my reflections and my truth, I may have made some false promises for the future. If that was my message, I truly am sorry for any pain this may have caused anyone to whom I am connected and I send them love.

These days, my promise is to myself, choosing to be mindfully aware, kind, honest, and loving in each moment I have. If I indeed make a conscious intention, I may catch myself living more in my truth and more in the moment. How? By choosing accountability, claiming it personally, and following through with action. I can then choose to invest tri-dimensionally, thus making a difference in the moment through simple acceptance. Allow me to further explain how this has manifested into enlightenment.

Watching people and hearing them differently from a soul's perspective gives you a different conclusion. We are all just trying to find a way to feel love, be loved, and find peace. We are all lost and we are all blind, but the God-source within wants us to be complete. Quite frankly, when we have those connecting moments of truth, so does our God-source. Powerful, loving energy sighs with us and rejoices in the love we are feeling in that single moment in time. That intimate experience, the kind you encounter when you fall in love or the experience of true peace and complete happiness, is a connection to the all that we are, the one true reason for our actual existence!

Also, in reflection on this subject, I have personally made the mistake of thinking that I need the aid of another person to lift my spirits and help bring me out of a funky mood. Not the truth at all! I need to take personal responsibility for taking care of my own sadness and heartaches. It is that single moment or second in time when you know beyond all truth that you are connected to something much bigger than your person. You are connected to an unconditional, never-ending pool of love and support that you can experience in every single second of your existence in body and spirit. This does not mean you don't need your "people" to support you in these times of personal growth. You really do, but not to save you, or lift you, or be responsible to enable you; just for support and a place to confide in.

When I was a child in church and the priest would say "never-ending eternal life," I would be almost overwhelmed and light-headed. It was scary for me as a child to even try to fathom that kind of life: How? Why? When? I could not wrap my small brain around never-dying eternal life, but it stuck with me and gave me foundation and hope that, in time, I might grasp that whole concept. It now excites me, gives me hope, encourages me, that even in the worst heartbreak or the worst separation, we can be mended, reborn, built new. Lifetime and lifetime again!

Maybe now, as I struggle with not being able to connect with my daughter on an emotional level or struggling to find my voice to communicate with friends from whom I have grown apart, my flesh and blood siblings with whom I have been struggling, my pain in finding my truth, and pain in working things out, the freedom for me in all of these issues is choosing to love them in the moments I have available, letting go of any expectations that may come from the separation, and then deliberately sending love and peace to the people from whom I have been separated. I need to stop asking myself why it had to be this way and start accepting the changes, not really needing to know the answers. I need to wish them love and good life, and peace in the moments of all the choices they make even if I do not consider them to be healthy or wise. I need to accept them and love them in the choices they have made without passing judgment! How hard is this? Well, being aware of this is a life-long process. I must say, I am getting better at recognizing it after years of practice!

It was in learning to accept others for who they are and accepting their decisions and choices without feeling responsible or judgmental that the Reiki love, the spiritual side of God and his legions of guiding angels and spirits came into play for me. I routinely ask for assistance in spirit form, and I open my human listening ears and accept the grace of this connection. I feel, and I listen, to the messages that come from the other side. This is the only way I am going to get a handle on understanding that even in my loneliness, I am never alone. I am not saying here that I will never be lonely. Please don't think that through all this growth, if I choose, I won't be lonely, because that is not the truth; but in my loneliness on this journey of self-discovery, what I will come to find is that I simply am never alone in spirit. Let me elaborate here a bit, if I may.

Things for me personally have changed. I bought into this package of self-truth and, at the time of writing this book, I am just coming into another phase. As I shut down my body and my practice mentally every end of the year and take a few months off, I return to Soul School for another semester or two. I do this through direction in meditation or a book that resonates with me at the time. During this time of reflection, my Reiki practice may evolve and change with different methods of healing through breath work or another medium tool channeled that has been added to my practice. What never ceases to amaze me, and a fact I have never questioned is that when a client is in session, there is always a specific healing, every single time.

This year has seen some surprises. I have been called out a few times by clients, and on each occasion, this calling out has been very necessary for the client. I made a promise to my God within that I would do that for anyone who needed me. Therefore, it is happening and I am acting or reacting to the calling out. This is not about me, but it is about the reaction I have on those calling me out. It has made me a finer-tuned machine in human and soul form, and therefore, my cognizance is responding in the moment. This is bigger than I am. It is a connection for the person and an aid in their personal journey!

The following are examples of channeling sessions and some of the experiences encountered and results obtained while working with various clients.

- I am quicker to recognize and confirm the uniqueness in strangers in the flesh who come into my life.
- I provide words their guides may have for them or a message to them from an angel or lost loved one, to confirm a fear or a validation and give them a loving message of hope, peace, love.
- I act out in a vocal way directed to them and for them, letting go of the thrill and the personal addiction of feeling so good

in sharing in the power of the moment that belongs to them on a personal soul level. I just get to be the messenger.

- I am able to enjoy and bask in gratitude to be asked to deliver the messages.

- I act on a feeling or stop in the moment to say a word, write a letter, or bring comfort to another person. I have always acted on this and receive instant validation that it was needed or that I am delivering a message of love.

It is a comfort to me that we are simply and truly all one moving mass, and we are simply and truly all very connected.

The Secret

Some people have a fear of touch or fear of love by loving acts. These acts could make them open for hurt and, if they are not careful, may expose their hidden secrets, leaving them open and vulnerable for rejection yet again. Some people are so sensitive to vulnerability and personal boundaries that they are on full alert of exposure. Another encounter that could further expose them or result in their "getting found out" or being discovered! Some people trust no one and actually build walls so high, you could never have a hope of climbing them. In fact, they don't even trust themselves, so they bury themselves in places they feel safe, but never find true peace. They have to break camp when another person they thought they could trust breaks that trust, and they have to move on to another fortress and start all over again. In those circumstances, I respect and love them in the brokenness they are comfortable living in and accept them as they are. In most cases, they are just asking for space.

This approach to life takes its toll. All these individuals crave is peace and love, and, in their own way, they set their own bars so high they are simply unattainable. This self-destruction becomes exhausting. Most people end up in sickness and physically debilitating illness, addictions, and avoidances, all because they do not know where to begin to find the love, peace, and acceptance they so desperately crave. But who are we to judge or want to help them change the lessons they are needing to learn?

On the other hand, if you are stuck and are asking for a hand-up to make changes in your life, then I suggest the secret! Start with having a secret inside you that you do not have to share with anyone, and then believe this to be your truth. Smell it, hold on to it, soak it into your being and join it with the unconditional love of the great I Am God-force that resides in your spirit. That force, in truth, is you in the flesh together with the universal loving energy and entities that exist in spirit form.

Buy into this truth! Know it, claim it, and become it! Having a secret makes you feel loved, special, cared for, even if the caring is coming from your own innerspace!

I know that this is a very hard concept to consider, and you may, at this time, not be able to wrap your life around all this information. I do know that this way of living, thinking, breathing, accepting, and existing may not be for everyone. I do know, and I cannot stress this enough, it is about being responsible for your deep-seated soul truth and acting on it with love and kindness, instead of avoiding any confrontation, ripples, fear, or change it may cause in the effect and the outcome of the entirety of your truth. We always have a choice!

Gratitude

Just think for a moment, if you could, about how it would help you grow if you couldn't see the trees for the forest instead of not seeing the forest for the trees. Same view, different perspective. If you could take each and every moment of your day and make it less about you and more about the need to listen, love, advise, choose to be alive, live in the moment, with the most amazing ingredient - the spice of all spices - the cause and the effect we are all seeking: gratitude! Such an overused word and yet seldom contemplated on a soul level.

Contemplate how much richer we would all be in our lives if we could just be grateful. How much more aware we would be, enabling us to listen and really hear what the world around us needs, and not just what we need.

If we could just stop and be thankful for our sheer existence and not expect another thing, how much more would we have within us to be able to give advice and share with the world? It is not easy to give up all the things we have worked so hard to gain and sacrificed so personally to achieve. Yet, in truth, that is what our honesty is calling us to do and be and see: sharing our wealth and our lives with the people who are put in our paths.

All of us have those moments of sheer magic. All of us have life-changing moments, teaching and molding us into who we ultimately chose to become. The secret is to not ever forget them. Build on them. Create an existence that tears down those walls and the resilience, the safety net you think you have around you, and make yourself more vulnerable so that you can be a healthier, stronger, more loving, giving force of light for the darkness that affects us all.

Who am I? I am one singular grain of sand in the masses of living beings with whom we are all connected! We together, united, can all make the difference if we choose living instead of existing. The requirements are quite simple: to say "yes." But making that switch can be most difficult to achieve. Change is not easy for anyone who has been fighting all their lives, trying to make a difference, to be heard, validated, and made to feel important by a parent who could be abusive or desperately lacked empathy due to the patterns and behaviors they were taught. There is no manual given to you at the hospital when you bring home the children to whom you gave birth. As a child, learning to fight off these rules of our world, being mandated, or suppressed, or being told not to speak created this fear factor lack of trust from an early imprint stage for me, and I expect for others, as well. Another insight: You don't have to stay in that place of fear! You can use the wisdom and the pain this experience taught you to rise above the imprint and to change the way you live in the freedom, wisdom, and knowledge the lesson brought you. You get to choose how your story ends. You get to choose how you learn from the lessons. Holding on to anger and resentment keeps you a prisoner.

You must understand this ingredient of forgiveness. Letting go of any hurts, memories of the hurt, and – most important – the desire for retribution is imperative. To do otherwise only results in more pain. You think it is validation and you think you may live long enough to see the suffering of those who inflicted this pain on you, but it is toxic waste and toxic energy that clog up the pores of your soul heart. Justice never comes in the end as the pain cycle just continues manifesting and disguising itself in addictions or habits that preoccupy your sacred soul space and shut you down in a subliminal, subtle, but steady way. Silence is not for everyone. It makes some people uncomfortable. Silence has become my best soul's learning tool.

People often say to me a leopard cannot change its spots, but has anyone ever considered this theory? The spots are a part of their appearance and their designated physical DNA, and it's a known truth that their fur may never change on the outside. We are speaking metaphorically of this leopard theory in human form. So, instead of judgment and revenge and justice in our hearts, we might look at that "leopard" with love. Maybe its spots can be softened through your heart and soul and the change that grows within you so you can see the spots differently.

If I thought this miracle could not exist, I would then be forced to believe there is no great "I Am" or God-energy. I would have to believe that there is no beautiful place to grow to and aspire to become all encompassing! The very existence of my soul will not allow me to think this way, not even for a second. I have chosen to believe people will change and grow, and love can manifest at all cost. The sun will shine in this world and the white light will continue to encourage goodness in all things. The sun will continue to shine through for me.

I choose to believe that a leopard can and will change its spots, maybe not in this lifetime, but it may eventually gain insight and knowledge that we are all one mass and we are growing into a loving consciousness.

Dark vs. Light

The dark side of things is not something I give much thought to anymore, not because I don't believe it is not in existence. Quite the contrary! I have experienced the dark side often in my life: struggling with an eating disorder they like to label "bulimia" and selfishly making unhealthy decisions for my personal gain, the need for instant gratification, borrowing items and not feeling a need to return them, lying to people, causing false hope, having hidden agendas, making astronomical mistakes; using people to gain things both materially and to gain favor in others. I do understand why these inflictions haunted me or created the enabler in me. I have had enough therapy, spanning some thirty years of my life on and off, to, yes, probably write another book on the theory of the choices and decisions I made. I know mostly it was all about the control I needed to have at the time of my poor choices. I also know it fed me, in a way, on a personal need or want. I felt entitled. Truthfully, it was simple self-gratification and self-destruction, all in the moment of making a choice.

I still have to be mindful of a sense of entitlement and can sometimes struggle with this in my ego state. That kind of thing never goes away. You will always have to feed some kind of giant in your body as long as the ego and the soul live together, but it is always so much better if you take a breath or a step back and think the choice through, and let the soul and the mind have a few seconds to discuss the action and then the result of your action. Sometimes the ego is stronger and wins, and you react and revert to old habits that satisfied you in the moment. Forgive yourself in that instant! That is imperative!

There are many things in my past of which I am not proud, dating back through many years of existence. I no longer waste my time flogging myself or trying to fix others to make all these things okay for me. Even if some of the choices I made in the dark side that I call "instant personal gratification" have caused people pain, I can honestly say I am truly and completely sorry for the inflictions that may have scarred them. I have made my peace with myself and my Maker, and I have started a new path; a gentler path.

In all my truth, I do still struggle with the addiction to food and the eating disorder. In all honesty, I embrace it and deal with it one day at a time instead of trying to fix that broken piece of me. I just embrace it, deal with it, and move past the moment; sometimes very successfully, other times not so much. But I am connected to the great I Am and He suffers along with me as I get it right this time - or not! It is just accepted, and it is simply another moment in time that allows me to see the pressures of my world and the instant gratification at my fingertips to buy into the dark side or stay firm in the light.

This should hit home with a few people who struggle along with me as I further explain dark energy or self-infliction. It is instant gratification! That I can tell you is my truth in the battle. It is a rush in the moment it happens, a feel good high, a secret. Yes, another one! It takes you away quickly to a place where there is no sunshine, just a bit of shame and remorse. It is a dark place of self-disgust and low self-esteem in the highest form. When this happens, the secret is your truth. In all ways, your truth will set you free and the tool is to forgive yourself in all your darkness so you can rise above, time and time again, into the light and into the love of self-forgiveness.

The dark side is instant gratification that feeds your deepest secrets and your deepest fears in one single, quick instant, and you will fight that dark side the whole time you are in existence. Yes, by choice! Now, you are getting the message of love and light. You get to choose. Is that not exciting? You can always choose to ask for forgiveness, starting with yourself and then those people whom you need to forgive.

Even writing this message of the dark side makes the temperature in this room of light and love change within me, around me. Please don't kid yourself. It is real and it exists. It should make the hair on the top of your head stand up and your eyes leak. It is a very real force gaining momentum daily, as some people choose to act on it, and envelope it, and cause pain and infliction, not only on themselves for the instant rush of gratification, but for the rush it gives them to cause pain to others.

As I said, it is real, so be aware and send it away often with a brush of love from your hand or a warm, loving thought, or even call on angels and loving energy to ask the presence to leave your state of mind and soul.

The following information details my experience with dark energy. It is not my wish to devote much time to this subject; however, I felt it necessary to touch on it. In my personal experience, I have decided not to feed the source.

Dark energy is instant, personal, worldly negative, unconstructive, restrictive, toxic, powerful, destructive energy. It can be gained in an instant, leaving in its wake shame and false hope. There is no power gained that remains in a positive light; only the power of overwhelming gloom and destruction. It is always, or in most instances, cold and damp. You could be in a room with a full fire roaring in a fireplace and still feel that damp feeling of despair. It is a shiver that never quite goes away and stays with you, lingering for a while. This feeling may give you glimpses of a memory or a past that is still real to the energy, even dating many centuries. It is where this energy chooses to stay stuck and does not move to the light. It does not mean the energy is always bad or malicious. Quite the contrary. This energy just chooses to hold on to the space or place, claiming in spirit the reality of the energy's worth and existence. Most times, it does not know or believe itself worthy of love and light. Or it simply has fear, regret, remorse, or guilt. Or it has not been able to heal or shed in a past life. In some instances, it doesn't even realize it has passed on and is just annoyed that a stranger has taken up residency in a physical body that is its homestead or space.

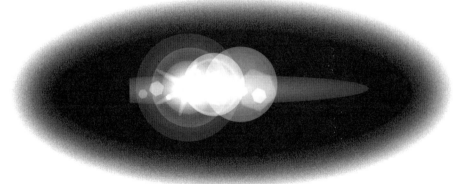

White energy takes time to manifest. It takes years and moments and life lessons to build and accumulate. It takes courage and sacrifices and wisdom that all take time to cultivate. Most of all, it takes huge self-control. It is so easy to give into the greed of the moment, as well as the desires of the heart.

The most awesome thing to remember - and this is truly enlightening! – is that if dark energy manifests anywhere near white energy, it is instantly burned up on the spot. It simply is the truth and the miracle of all miracles. Darkness can never, ever, exist if there is light!

I have noticed if I pay attention, the signs of struggle in the world share two forces of energies. Instant demand feeds the instant craving. An example of this is the expectations and the demands that people put on service. I have a suspicion that the employees at my favourite coffee shop are timed to offer faster service. If this is, indeed, a fact, the pressure would be immense for the workers. That makes me sad! The way people say "I am sorry" in a normal conversation because they may need to bend your ear on a personal subject matter or something they want to share, they are actually saying they are sorry for taking up your time. Ordinary people and their high expectations choose to sometimes not take personal accountability, quickly blaming and bullying instead of claiming and sharing decent interaction between us in acts of kindness.

We have, as I like to say, a window to the world and many instant moments. We have free reign and information at our fingertips that can be a powerful tool of destruction and violation.

On the positive side, how fortunate we are to be able to communicate with someone we love by instantly being attached to them on Skype or FaceTime! How awesome it is to be able to speak to a sick family member half way around the world! Or talk to your child away at school, or your partner away on business. I truly hope I never, ever stop embracing what all these gifts can be and do for me. I hope I am always wise to the power of instant communication and technology. At the same time, I truly hope we never stop talking face to face and heart to heart in the midst of all this instant quick connection. I am aware that balance is more important than ever, and we must use all these gifts in moderation and still make time to share in body and soul.

I am super excited about something I just learned and truly want to share it before I forget it. Retention is not my strong point. I honestly mean it. So many daily details do not stick in my short term memory; I know it has something to do with being a spiritual filter for so many people who feel safe telling me things. There seems to only be enough room in that headspace for this work most of the time. I have also come to know that the information I receive does not belong to me; therefore, I do not retain what is not mine to keep. Personally, and honestly, it used to bother me not feeling comfortable at times talking about important world events, or people, places, and things. Now, it is just accepted within me and around me, all due to just being okay with "who I am, wherever I am."

Do you ever feel this way? If so, I have come to believe it is normal. Our worlds, our environments, our mandates are so huge every day, with more and more expectations, timelines, personal accountability. The hours we work are hard and long, and the available play time while in the work stages of our lives encompasses less and less time as we see the world and the priorities of our obligations to family and work. What time, if any, left over for friends and self takes a very sneaky, subliminal back seat.

I believe it is because our brains are on overload, overdrive, and burnout! I have stopped feeling guilty if I personally forget a birthday or an appointment that had to be changed for whatever reason. I work on the structure of my day that lies before me and I adjust accordingly to the time and the moments I am living in, trying to not get caught up in the past. I have an amazing quote taped beside my computer. It is a quote from an Ancient Chinese Philosopher by the name of Laozi (Lao-tzu). It states: "If you are depressed, you are living in your past. If you are anxious, you are living in your future. If you are at peace, you are living in the moment." I love this! It registers truth and peace every single time I read it. It is like heart candy!!!

Spiritual Housecleaning

I wish to share a secret with you and a story that goes like this.

I have been struggling with a situation that I have CLAIMED. Yes, I capitalized the word "CLAIMED" FOR A REASON! I took on a person and tried to fix her. For over six years now, I have tried several ways to suggest and advise, listen and counsel. This person, for whatever reason, cannot seem to grow the way I FEEL IS CONSTRUCTIVE FOR HER. Again, I CAPITALIZED THIS FOR YOUR ATTENTION! The moment of growth for me was actually vocalizing the truth of this situation and cutting the cords of the emotional attachment to this person. The energy and frustration and time I was putting into this person far surpassed the amount of time and growth I was putting into any other person I have around me. For any other client I have worked with, I just use the Gifts I was given, put myself in work mode, channel or mediate from the other side for them with a message that does not belong to me. I fill them with love, and light, and healing Reiki energy and send them on their way. Yes, I have cried with clients in the massive healings I have witnessed. Yes, I also have healings when my clients heal. The difference with this long-term commitment is just that with my clients, I do not emotionally attach myself to their lives or energy. They are never more to me than a client whom I have come to respect, and the only emotion I attach to these acquaintances is love and the ability to know they need help and are seeking to be whole. With this other person, I was trying to fix and trying to solve the world for them. I was claiming them emotionally and I was being disappointed continually and personally regarding their choices.

Letting go of and recognizing my part in trying to change this person gave me the insight to stop trying to enable them. This wisdom was the truth I needed in this experience and it stopped my frustration. It was their choice to be "lying dormant in a stagnant, non-changing situation." Simply, this person was not growing in the way I expected them to grow. In that moment of awareness and lightheartedness, I was free. And here is the key: FREE was the moment I addressed this issue in truth, out loud with my vocal cords, saying the words, "I AM DONE." I chose not to give this situation one more ounce of my expended energy that was trying to control, not feed. On the contrary, I just cut it off. I cut off the emotions, not the person. Here is the good news: You can still love the person and all the good things about the person. The list of positive attributes is usually a very long list if you look deep in the soul of the being. In this case, this person has a huge list of positive, loving qualities. This person is creative, beautiful, kind, humorous, and trustworthy. I have chosen to concentrate on sending powerful, loving energy, and I refuse to state any negative opinion on a personal level.

If I feel my personal frustration rising to the top and wanting to lash out because I feel personal about this person, I take a breath and rethink my answer. I need to grow bigger, and I will never be able to move past this and find my freedom in this situation if I don't actually practice what I am preaching. In all honesty, this has been a challenge and I have had a few dark days around this whole situation, but they are becoming fewer and fewer and I am higher up the mountain. So, if a problem is mine, I address it. It's that simple.

The miracle, and yes, there is one for this situation, is I have reached a stage where I have not one emotional shred left over, not even a spiritual hangover. I am able to address this person with a clear heart and a free spirit. Yes, it was that instant – that moment of truth - when I felt an emotional, healthy detachment from this person. Any expectations were wiped out like a clean chalkboard, like the content of that good book I just read, or that movie I just watched, forgetting everything but the plot. I simply let go of what I was trying to save, and in that reaction to the action, I actually re-saved myself, setting myself free! Imagine that kind of freedom! Imagine with one truthful powerful moment, following through and claiming your freedom and, most importantly, your peaceful inner space.

Spiritual house cleaning is good for your soul; it unclogs all your junk in your trunk, making room for new life purpose, new creative energy, new life lessons, awareness, and finally, seeing fully your own purpose!

Like any healthy choice, it takes time to buy into the lifestyle and commit to the choice. It can easily become overwhelming as when you start to think positive and healthy, consciously there seems to be an overwhelming, mechanical brake system internally that says to you and your body, "Hey! We have worked too hard and too long, working and creating you to live a certain way and have created a system within you that works." Even if the system is built on flaws, it works and your body will always resist this new method, system, spiritual changes, as well as nutritional changes and, yes, any type of foreign exercising, too. Your body, your mind, and your soul will resist all these changes that are going to require retraining and hard work.

Spiritual Advisement

Let's talk a bit about spiritual advisement. We are backtracking a few years now so bear with me as we go back a bit in my history - about 20 years. I was kind of having innerspace itch. It started with questioning my existence.

I really believe and I have come to know personally that coincidence is not a word to which I give any merit. That is not to say it is not a word. I just don't ever believe anything is a coincidence. I was at Mass on my knees "praying" and a lovely lady tapped me on the shoulder while I was in prayer and whispered in my ear, "Tracey, the spirit spoke to me and said that you have to come to the Abundant Life seminars. It is only a six-week course and you really need to come. I have been asked to pick you and you really have to come." Well first, I was in prayer. How bold of her! And secondly, this woman was, in my mind, absolutely certifiable! I turned and said, "I will think about this and pray about this." So, pray I did, and think I did, and I went kicking and screaming all the way, saying to myself with arms crossed the first night, "This hooky kooky stuff is really not my thing: raising hands and falling in the spirit." At that point in my journey I could not personally relate to this type of worship! The spirit world was about to teach me a different perspective!

After the first night I was not sold, and the next week either. I sat rigid and sour-faced through two weeks of what I thought to be maple syrup sweetness of people pouring out their innerspace and guts and strewing them all over these strangers. I did, however, love the music. I felt compelled and drawn by it, soaked it in, and started to feel a bit of something foreign to me. The Holy Spirit was working its magic! About the third week into the seminars, something changed and I actually started to kind of buy into this abundant, charismatic, unseen energy in the room. Our small group included a woman I had never met before, and we were growing at about the same rate. We were actually in the same grade of Soul School. We quickly grew connected and developed a bond in a spiritual manner we still have to this day. That is what happens when you are drawn in spirit. Although the flesh may change and the relationship in the flesh may change due to ego compatibility, the spirit parts continue to love the spirit form of the person forever. It's such a great way to love a person without personal conditions. After all, we are truly born and called to love. One of my favorite sayings is, "We are called to love. We are not called to like. To like is always a personal choice."

In and around the fifth week of this series of seminars, I started to really hear the spirit speaking to me through the leader of our small group. She was gifted and shone from the inside out. She had the gift of prophesy, and when she spoke you could hear the actual voice of God. I was taught what the gifts of the spirit were in this new abundant lifestyle and also what the fruits of the spirit were that extended from the gifts. I personally asked for three. The first gift I asked for was to be drenched in the gift of Love; the second gift I asked for was to understand Wisdom in the spiritual sense of the word. Another fruit of a gift I asked for was to speak in Tongues. I wanted to speak directly to the God-source. I wanted to speak a pure language of love to Him from my heart. without any type of intervention.

At that time, I still believed in two sources of power: God (good) and Devil (evil). I no longer think this way. That is not to say that evil does not exist in energy form. I do believe it does. I just choose not to give the dark side any shred of personal power. I sometimes think when you walk in the light, the dark side just cannot come close to your light. It combusts and dissipates. It's as simple or as complicated as we choose. I choose to not give power to an ego-selfish source that is instant and self-destructive. When I speak in spirit, and sometimes, to be honest, I don't use the gift given to me as much as I should, it is an instantaneous connection to my God within my innerspace and in the space that surrounds me.

As I grew in this new spiritual essence, understanding and digesting these gifts of the Spirit, I grew inside my innerspace. And honestly, I was actually very grateful for the gentle prods I received in the flesh through real life, dedicated angels like the woman who suggested I attend, who just acted as an agent for God. I fought my ego at the time, but came to awareness through maturity in my lessons, able to identity her beautiful soul spirit.

I will take a moment to explain the effects of the other gifts I asked for. The gift of Love was given to me in the last session of the seminars. They had a Celebration Mass for all the people who took the course and there was a part in the Mass where we could go up and a prayer team would lay hands on us, and we were filled or laid in the spirit. Most people fell and seemed to be having some kind of personal, out-of-body experience. It was rather unnerving actually to watch. When it came time for our row to have this experience, a new friend whom I had acquired in my group nudged me and out I went to receive what it was I was supposed to receive. To say I was nervous was an understatement. I had no idea that what was about to happen to me would plant a seed so deeply embedded in my soul, I would never be able to return to my old ways of life. Had I had the insight at the time, I might not have gone forward. In saying this, we still have a choice and I chose the unknown.

When the team started to pray over me, I was filled with a raw, emotional, pure love I could barely contain in my body. It was bigger than me, wiser than me, and filled me with awe. I was laid in the spirit and then my heart started to really hurt. Actually, the person who prayed over me later confessed that she thought she might have to call an ambulance as she suspected at the time I might be having a heart attack. She, in some ways, was correct. Every single pain I have ever experienced in heartache form was being physically pulled from my heart. As it left me, my broken heart squashed several times over the years in life and lessons, all loss and grief were gone. My broken, patchwork heart was replaced with a brand new heart. That is how I can explain it, and the new heart was so full of love, and forgiveness, and hope, and life. It still is that way. I honestly and truly believe with all my heart that I was granted the gift of pure love that day.

What has always fascinated me is that I still get to keep the stories, and the memories, and the lessons, and I use them in my life to this day, to share or connect with a new client who is a broken person, someone who may have gone through a similar tragic lesson. How can you share if you have not experienced the lesson? How can you connect and help someone see another way if you have not walked in the shoes they walk in? The miracle for me is the emotional attachment or pain of the memory or scar tissue is gone. It's just a story without an attachment emotionally, so it has no pain. The most awesome thing about addressing and getting rid of the emotional attachment is blissful freedom in the highest degree.

The gift of Wisdom was also given to me in that moment. It has been a silent, steady channel that flows when someone asks a question. This powerful gift of Universal Wisdom always has an answer, and not just a simple answer. It is wisdom and it is direct and accurate as it has only one agenda: the truth to the questions asked. It is instant, and it is accurate, and it has nothing to do with me or my personal knowledge on a subject matter. It has to do with Divine Wisdom and how I am the filter, and the tool, and the channel.

Sometimes, I tell people I am one soul in one body. If you picture a sand beach, I am one grain of sand on that beach. I can remain one grain of sand and still experience a beautiful life, choosing my personal lessons of love and grace. However, it has been my journey to know that I can still be that one grain of sand, true in my identity, and, at the same time, allow myself to share with all human contact if I choose. I can also reach out further, giving myself permission to invite divine collective groups of energy to work with me and channel knowledge and gifts to the world through me. I am then aware and available for the masses, seeking connection to them. In addition, they will be gifted with universal, divine, loving, wise knowledge. This wisdom is a constant; these gifts are a constant; healing and growing and changing are constant. This is living fully if you choose this way of life. If not, you will exist anyway, and you will continue to find ways to bring you joy. The choice for me is a richer, more abundant lifestyle. I have mentioned before that this way of life is not something everyone chooses. It can tend to be a lonely life, but I can promise you with all my soul, you are never, ever alone in the spirit world, which has an endless population. Your internal richness will grow and blossom within your innerspace.

I believe that if we accept who we are in our innerspace, this place and space have a lifetime warranty and guarantee us a free soul travel ticket to a new lesson or life experience. This freedom allows me to spend less time in my ego state. This takes practice, it takes commitment, and it takes a lifetime to develop. I totally believe in this investment. It is more valuable to date than any material thing I have ever received.

So, after a few months of this new abundant life, I was in love with the honeymoon phase of falling in love with my new spiritual essence and the awakening I had experienced. Honestly, when people say you fall in the spirit and are drunk by it, this statement rings true! You really do get a high or are simply drunk in it. The overwhelming urge to fall in love with nature or to hug a stranger is so present that you feel the emotional and physical effects.

Receiving gifts and fruits of the spirit is like falling in love in a relationship, but it is the kind of relationship that happens with spirit and self, i.e. falling in love with your God-source and yourself in the flesh. This type of relationship is soul based, not ego based.

Several months into this new lifestyle, I started to share my gifts with a person I felt would understand what I was experiencing. In sharing my experience with her, she was not very supportive. In fact, she basically told me she thought I was experiencing signs from a source that was not of God, meaning she thought I was getting satanic information and guidance.

You can well imagine my utter shock, fear, and displacement and what might be going on in and around my innerspace, having been told that I was not acting in a God-focused and loving way, but rather gaining wisdom and advice from quite the opposite. I was devastated and heartbroken and started to second-guess my intentions.

To this day, I will never forget the feelings that developed around me when I hung up the phone. But a voice, the very voice that has always been with me in my heart at these times, came to me and advised me to pick up the phone and call another person who was a spiritual advisor. This beautiful being led me and listened to me. She advised me of many things. We exchanged Reiki and she led me to great meditational skills and seminars. She directed me to the light and she directed the light to me by teaching me to trust my channeling gifts. She was kind and she had a brilliant mind and a contagious laugh. SHE saved me in a sense and gave me the gift of my human pendulum, which I use and share to this day as a guide when my ego-mind is making direction murky. She was definitely a gift of divine, perfect timing. Savor what you have and share with hungry people who really want to know, to grow or learn, to heal, and to experience life. She was a divine gift to me, and she and the wisdom and the mentorship gave me bigger wings to fly and wider feet to find firmer foundation. I will forever be grateful and can only hope to become as enlightened on my journey and my quest to help heal the wounded of the world. I say this with wisdom, honesty, and maturity.

When you heal, I also heal. We will heal together, as one mass united.

For several years after this experience, I must say I developed slowly, coasted, dabbled, and encouraged others to find their way and their truth. It was not until I finally met and fell in love with a healthy person that I realized that I was actually becoming healthy myself and making better choices. It seems when that happens and you are wise enough to pick healthy or healthy picks you, you have all the components to make this manifest quicker.

SECTION THREE

Experiences to Share and Learn From

The Very, Very Bad Day

I would like to take you along with me and share a very overpowering day. It was a Thursday - a nothing special kind of day - but it started off, as some people suggest, on the wrong foot...or on the wrong side of the bed. I was running behind terribly and was not ready for the lovely ladies with whom I car pool, and I kept them patiently waiting for me for an extra five whole minutes. I was out of sorts and grumpy. I am sure you have all experienced one of those kinds of days.

When I arrived at work that morning, the reception area was taped off in yellow caution tape. There was a huge, noisy lift inside the entrance way and a massive wall mural being installed. I want you to know that the space I am privileged to work in is normally big, beautiful, and quiet. I am terribly spoiled with the best office in the building.

It just so happened the same day there was a huge sale/store winter clearance right next door to the reception door. Already agitated like the high-speed cycle on a spin washer, I felt the entire day starting to snow ball and increase in intensity. I could feel my human emotions, stretching like a rubber band on the verge of snapping.

Interesting enough, that day I also had a few intensely emotional universal things happen from a spiritual aspect. I had three visitors that day in spirit. One visitor came to see me in spirit through his daughter. He was a very dear, close friend of mine whom we lost to brain cancer. He was an interesting man with a rather twisted sense of humor! His daughter had never come to see me at my office before, nor has she stopped in since; however, on that day of all days, she decided to come in and bring her two darling sons. I could feel her daddy smiling behind her and could feel the connection in his spirt as we talked about him and cried, both loving and emotional tears together as we talked.

The second encounter in spirit that day was through a dear co-worker. We share a similar journey, so we often talk about past loved ones and share an invitation for them to join us in conversation as we spend time together. She must have had a sense that I was needing a bit of extra love and came down and shared her lunch with me. Her father, who passed to the other side a few years ago, decided to show up with some words of love for her. It just so happened that it was his birthday. He had kind, loving messages of hope and inspiration for her, and we were both touched to the core that he came for a visit on our lunch break.

The third visit nearing the end of the day was a very big surprise, as a young man I met as a customer with a broken zipper came in. I have a bit of history with this young man's mother, knowing her as an acquaintance in the town where we live. She passed to the other side a few years ago. As this young man walked into my office, he was on a mission to discuss her and we spent a few minutes inviting her into our conversation. He left with an uplifted, happy heart as well as the confirmation he was looking for. Gaining this truth, he felt his heart open to the knowledge he was able to gain thought this connection, confirming all he needed to know to make the choices he was contemplating.

To say this was a normal day for me, in all honesty, was not far from the truth. I have many days that are multi-faceted and change from one emotion to another in a single heart-beat. This day, however, challenged me both physically and emotionally. It seemed to be overwhelming in so many ways.

The reality of the physical world and the obstacles that caused some annoyance that day, combined with the visits of love and hope and messages from the spiritual world, indeed kept me humbled and confirmed the fact that I am a human being destined to have a few days like this that seem to unsettle me in both the physical world and the spiritual world in which I live daily.

And then the day was done and, as we say every day, "All in a day's work," but this day was a kick-in-the-pants kind of day and that resulted in an attitude adjustment. I went home that night in an abnormally uneasy state. Emotionally and physically exhausted, with a strong-willed ego mindset, I felt like I had just taken on and slayed several dragons. As I am relaying these feelings in words, it brings to mind a dear friend with whom I have shared the first draft of this book. He was trying to understand what I was trying to say and confessed to me that he is mostly a logical, "black and white" thinker. He said the following: "Soul School. Is this a term regarding the structure of your Reiki training or some other spiritual philosophy you have been exposed to, or is this a 'Traceyism' that describes your own spiritual journey? If it is a 'Traceyism' (and I mean that with respect), then it leads me as a reader to say 'tell me more.'"

He was asking me questions about things he wanted to know more information on. His inquires allowed me to take my "Traceyism" to heart and process the whole day's experience by sitting back and becoming aware, taking it all in and letting go of the lessons that brought me pain or discomfort. In hindsight, it may have been a kinder option for me to allow the flow of the day to happen without trying to control the course of it. In reflection, I allowed myself acceptance. What followed was grace in the lessons, sprinkled with love and gratitude. My spiritual teachers from the other side rejoiced in the wisdom they brought me that day. They are constantly trying to teach me that work still goes on, teaching me to work around the obstacles, and claiming only the lessons that belong to me, as well as accepting love where and when it is given.

It has been a constant truth for me that when I accept love and goodness from the helping hands that wish to support me, respect me, and accept me (like my carpool girls), I am allowing them into my boundaries, giving them permission to share their collective wisdom and gifts they too have gathered and feel the need to share. IT'S NOT ALL ABOUT ME ALL THE TIME! Listening with my heart and hearing on a spiritual level allows me the grace to open myself up to vulnerable places, so that others may offer healing and heal along with me.

Yes, this could have been said in not so many words, but that is what we do when we share. We add all the ingredients so that you can come along and experience the intimacy and personal journey with me.

What did I learn on that Thursday? That we are all connected and there is no way we can be successful by doing it all alone. We need a team of people who are committed to being in love and loving, kind and courageous. I also need to learn again that every day I have to re-commit to human error, expecting nothing and trying not to judge. This can be very difficult, but the spirits that connect to me say, "Tracey, try to think with heart instead of the ego."

Pay it Forward

On a lovely evening a few days later, one of my oldest friends called to see if I wanted to go for a walk after work with her. We met the following evening and we caught up. This friendship is older than most of my friendships as we have grown up together. There is about a 14-year age gap between us. We seem to share our growth differently: sometimes she needs me; other times I need her. She says I teach her things. I say she accepts me without judgment and conditions. I can be my real self with her, and she with me. She is a very gifted person and lives from her heart and soul. She is an old soul in a young body. She is beautiful inside and out, so it did not surprise me on the walk when she proceeded to share with me a story about the previous day.

She was in a line-up in the grocery store buying water. She was buying just the water as it was a good price. She noticed the woman in front of her, who was purchasing a quantity of lower priced, no name products, and noticed they were staples – items she needed to live - no extras. The sales clerk told the woman the cost and as she fumbled around in her purse for the money, she said, more to herself, "I don't have enough money." She then proceeded to take things off the conveyor belt. My friend turned to the sales clerk and said, "Please add this to my bill." The woman started to cry, and my friend said, "Please do not do that. I cannot handle that. Please stop crying and just some day when you are able, just pay it forward." The woman said she would and they both went their separate ways. My friend said it made her think of me and that is why she called me on the way home.

What a beautiful gesture of pure love! How that action may have turned that woman's whole day around, providing for her a small ray of sunshine to lighten her heartache! I am grateful for my friend and will be every day for the rest of my time here.

I would really love to write the countless letters I have shared between loved ones, asking and seeking, as well as clients asking and seeking validation. In saying this, I have had conversations with a few beautiful soul connections who have agreed to be a part of this innerspace journey we are sharing together. Our united goal is to try and educate the masses. We want to try and share with people everywhere that we all have this ability to be open, honest, and truthful, but it would be like my spiritual advisor who so wisely said, "Never throw your pearls to the sow," which actually means if it is sacred to you or belongs to someone else, it should be cherished and protected.

I have permission to share with you from the following light workers, and I would like to start with a lady by the name of Carol. She and I met one day a few years ago in shop in a town called Lexington, Michigan. Carol was doing readings that day, and I was lucky enough to have had a reading done by her. It was not the type of reading I was very familiar with, as she channels for a spirit guide by the name of Jacob. His spirit belongs to a collective group of energies that have not been physically present on the earth since the time of ice (in his words). He says in the time he was a medicine man, and he and his group witnessed destruction by what he calls "the tall ones." He says that they have returned here in this time to aid us as he says humanity needs them more than ever. Carol shared with me that Jacob has presented her with visions of future destruction and chaos that are troubling for her and it breaks her heart to watch the pain and fear. On the other hand, Jacob has also shared with her visions of light, love, and the beauty of lessons learned.

My channeling encounters from Jacob are encouraging, peaceful messages of wisdom and love. They always make me feel supported, respected, cherished, and enriched. The group he is connected with when he speaks through Carol heart to heart always gives me tools and purpose, and he speaks of them as one, not a single spirit. To call it humbling to have this vast amount of love poured into you, not to mention the collective wisdom, well, it's more like Prana - food for my entire being. What is even more interesting about my connection with Carol is that she says I always call when she needs me. She says it is always so empowering for her that Jacob seems to communicate to me when I need to call her and help her heal something she needs help with, so we work on and with each other in these phone calls. A huge healing happens at these times and it seems to be enough to carry us over until the next time I hear her soul calling me. I know Jacob is grateful that we are keeping his host as healthy as possible, healing together. He has told me she needs what we share together and he endearingly calls me "Little One" and says, "You have much to give and offer the world." When I called and enquired about writing this section and asked Carol to check with the collective group, she was covered in validation and they seemed to be sending the message that, indeed, it was not from an ego space and that, indeed, to proceed and be open. When I end my phone calls with Carol, I have another full tank to carry on and to do the work I am called to. She makes me happy and she is all about honesty, integrity, truth, and love.

In 2009, I met an amazing woman in London, Ontario at a phychic fair. She had beautiful energy and glowed from her innerspace, her eyes, and her smile. Her laugh made me laugh and we connected in a way that soul people do. She just became a part of my collective group of light workers. Her name is Beverly Stephan and the reason I have added her full name is because she is the artist medium who channeled the cover of this book for us. I can tell you this may turn into a bit of a testimonial, and so it should with the gift I received in her session and my personal experience.

I did book a session and sat down across from Beverly. She took my hands and started to collectively gather my spirit guides, angels, and animal guides. She took paper and a combination of different paint colors, folded the paper and proceeded to channel my guides into the paper with the help of her guides. She opened it and showed me what materialized! I still have this magnificent, one-of-a-kind, personal art reading framed in my Reiki room where I can have a visual of all the workers helping me in my sacred space.

Beverly and I have stayed as connected as the day we met over the past years. There have been no changes between our souls, just constant love and validation that brings us both home when we connect. And yet, as I say this, there have been changes and validations in our work and lives. I recently sent two connected, beautiful clients I adore toward Beverly. The wife wanted to buy her husband an art reading as a gift. They, too, had an amazing experience. So, as I was, as Beverly would say, contemplating on the book and listening for my inner guides or direction recently, Beverly's name and face appeared in my heart. I usually wait for this validation when it happens, as it does often. I wait for it to keep coming. After the third time of the same name and face appearing, added to a feeling of what the person needs or the message for me to act on, I respond. This time with Beverly, it was direct and the message was "Send her an e-mail right now. Tell her you are writing a book and ask her if she would like to design the cover." Her response was immediate, within a very few minutes. She said, "OMG Tracey! The spirit is validating this all over my body. Yes!" We talked about the process and how this was going to happen and together, we would work on this. The most interesting thing for me was before she even said yes, "my Joe" told me that he had a vision of me on his vision board, standing in a room holding my book and speaking to a group of people. I closed my eyes and was in the room, and in my hand was the book. The cover was a white one with one of Beverly's spiritual paintings on the cover. She is a blessing and a gift. Beverly is an authentic, divine artist and medium for spirits who work in conjunction with us from the other side.

She called me on May 18th at 7:00pm. It is an honest statement when I speak for both of us on our technical gifts, that it took a few moments for the two of us to get our act together, connecting to Skype so we could both watch the fascination from the other side of the spirit world unfold in front of us in the mystery that surrounds her gifted hands and open heart.

We sat and opened in prayer, Beverly first setting the stage for the other side to channel through her, and then she asked me to pray holding the manuscript close to my heart. She asked me to pray for the intentions and the calling of my heart and soul. She asked me to speak with her in spirit form prayer. That experience alone was beyond beautiful! We then proceeded to work, me asking for the guides to come through and her doing her gifted work. In the first picture, I immediately saw Archangel Michael and his purple angel wings. Big, bold, and beautifully divine and protective! Other guides, animals and angels started to manifest. The second was just as powerful as the first and totally different. The third, in time after meditation, I realized was all three combined. The colors are beyond words and there are so many messages of love and support in this third presentation. It is the one that I chose for the cover of Innerspace. It is personal and it is beautiful. It is the confirmation I was looking for and I have this incredible team of spirit guides and teachers in all forms involved in this mission of connection for all.

Beverly is a gifted soul sister who believes in this work and in the gifts we have been given to share with the world around us. I am thrilled to have had this experience with her and love her deeply. I am proud of the warrior and the child in Beverly, who encourages me with humor and human behavior to continue to be the person I am in flesh as well as in spirit. You will enjoy her gifts as much as I will every time I look at the cover of Innerspace. You will claim something personal of your own - I just feel that in my heartspace.

Beverly's Mantra: Live Light, Be Light, Spread Light

I have been so fortunate in my practice to have met some very powerful people, soul workers, and human beings. We seem to have a connection that none of us really comprehends on a human level. We have just come to accept it for what it is. How comforting to know we are always learning, loving, and growing, even from distance! Is that not exciting?

These powerful women, in particular, make me so proud. They are both proud, no nonsense, incredible women of honour and integrity. They are both on a mission to better the world around them, take care of the ones they cherish, and be as healthy as possible, creating a healing within. Who in all wellness would not want to grow bigger, better, and stronger, being connected with beings who are empowering in this way of existence? For me, these two particular women encourage me, help me, and, most importantly, accept me for who I am, loving me enough to not ask for anything extra, including time and friendship on a human level. They love me completely without conditions. Does that mean they don't want a friendship? Not at all! If time allowed, they would be the first ones to ask for a coffee or dinner date. They just somehow know that to have a piece of anything I have to give right now is all about connecting on a soul and personal level without asking me for any more than what I can give them. How freeing!

This brings to mind another dear heart I mentioned earlier. We will name her Sunshine. She truly is my sunshine and she honestly is like special growth serum for me. She is beautiful, wise, and stunning. I adore you too, Sunshine, for all the reasons, seasons, and times we have shared and will continue to share. During our process, I believe we live time and time again.

These women are my heart circle. They sacrifice sometimes the need for more of me and allow me to breathe and grow and be all I need to be for the masses who still need what I can give them. I love this so much!

I have also come to another realization, and it has been very recent actually. It was my fifty-ninth birthday and it, as always, was an overwhelming day for me. It always reminds me how loved I am, and it was interesting to see how exhausted I was from receiving so much all day. I was gifted with so many kind thoughts, words, cards, messages, flowers, and a chocolate-covered fruit bouquet that was too pretty to eat from my sweet sister, the second youngest, a gentle angel soul. It was great to share with all the people I work with. My sweetheart sent me flowers from him and his mother. How can a women's heart not melt when you get flowers from the man you adore and the woman who bore him? Come on! That would melt even the crustiest heart. It makes me smile, but at the same time, it was exhausting to experience this kind of affection and validation.

Another beautiful soul I have just started getting to know came by my work, brought me flowers, sent me the funniest e-card I had ever received, and offered to drive me home. When this woman smiles her whole body lights up, and right in front of my eyes she becomes an angel. She is calming and gentle, and as I babbled all the way home, she listened and she supported all the things happening in my life. She said, "Tracey, you are fortunate." And yes, that would be the one word I think hit the spot that day.

I did have a nagging moment though, and it was one of those moments when you realize you have had a spiritual growth spurt. I promised myself that when I wrote this book, I would be honest as well as kind.

I had a few people say in their greetings to me that they missed me. As honoured and touched as I was by their comments, I realized that I did not miss these connections in my innerspace truth. I very seldom use the words "I miss you" anymore. I have grown to a place of acceptance of how busy people are, wrapped up in their lives, and how much pressure the world puts on people to be available for relationships - past, present, future. I have come home in my heart, and I am committed to the people in my life who do not expect me to be anything more or anything less on those days when I am curled up in my pajamas or sweat pants with hair in a ponytail and no makeup. This freedom in me has allowed me to love the people who have been in my life, my entire life. I have a magic photo album in my heart that I bring out and remember sending them love in the moments they were my friends and sacrificed themselves for my personal growth. They never die, and those beings of love and light are just carried along with me, not judging either of us and accepting and sending them love and light. You see, they never leave me. Those friends and connections supported my growth, carrying me to a new level of enlightenment. The conversations are as fresh as the moments and days when they happened.

One dear heart, with whom I travelled and sang for years, entwined in each other's lives, was on the phone with me in a rough patch just after my second relationship ended and we could smell the moment, and she said to me, "You always go check it out and then when you get to the other side you call me over when its safe." An angel friend, she gave me shelter when I needed it and was rebuilding a new life. Her darling son relinquished his bedroom for me - his own idea - so I could have place to grieve. Another lent me money and when I went to pay it back, he did not remember lending it to me, but simply said, "Pay it forward." And so, we do pay it forward. So, for me to say "I miss you, too" – the truth is, I do not miss you simply because I never, ever forget you and you are a part of my innerspace. You have all given me wings and space to fly. Fortunate is not a big enough word some days.

I might add here that if you are missing something or someone, take some time to contemplate who, why, and what it is in your core that you are missing and make changes in your life so that you can fill the hole and heal in the ways you may feel need the emotional adjustments by your personal actions. Journal, seek out, and make time connecting or just accepting that people change, move on, and grow in different directions. Face your own truth and, in your honesty, you will have a healing of such magnitude that you will rejoice in the knowing that it is your job and your destiny to find your own wholeness in any way you need to find it, and then to just share with the world, paying it all forward.

San Miquel de Allende

I recently had another epiphany, a life-changing moment. You would think by now that I would be used to this type of learning process. Strangely, you never get used to the changes. It's like you are learning things all over again, in an entirely new, pretty package some days and a not-so-pretty package on other days. The learnings that leave you feeling like you are picking thistles out, like you have rubbed up against a Mexican cactus, are the ones that sometimes leave the stinger in and it takes a few processing days for them to work their way out of your skin. This is the one I want to talk about today.

We had just had an opportunity to visit dear friends in Mexico. When I say Mexico, it was rural, so not some nice, warmly tucked away resort at the beginning of your journey. We landed smack in the middle of a very busy Mexico City Airport. This learning was a whole different experience with people, food, and culture. We went to San Miguel de Allende, SMA for short as everyone calls it. Upon arrival, we rented a car and proceeded on, driving to the hidden treasure of our destination in the middle of the mountains, about a three- to four-hour drive.

I was absolutely stunned and in shock, witnessing my ignorance of the culture of another country unfold. In truth, every kind of action and uncomfortable interaction my eyes could greedily hold occurred in the first fifteen kilometres past the airport. It was like watching a movie, but feeling the emotion of being there in person. Parks for kids that looked like dog parks for us; garbage and furniture strewn on the sides of the highway and intercity roads; bicycles renovated into moving rickshaws with plastic wrap around them; vehicles that were so lopsided I was mesmerized, wondering how they did not tip over onto their sides, and we are talking full-out, huge trucks.

The roads were treacherous, and I was comforted that Joe could so quickly adapt to the driving. In no time, he fit right in and maneuvered expertly. The key piece of advice from my wise and wonderful partner: "You adapt and become one of the natives." SO true! So wise! It is literally the reason I am writing this today. We survived living with the mass by being one of the mass and conforming to the way they think and the way they drive in their environment and country. This was an extremely humbling lesson for me. Joe did not let fear consume him. He just adapted to the driving force of the mass to which he was connected and politely conformed. We could learn so much by instant action of what it actually means to say "survival of the fittest" - in body, in mind, and in a soul's attitude of acceptance.

We did have some bumps along the way but, in all fairness, that would actually happen in a strange country and neither of us spoke Spanish, so the navigation was a challenge. Thank God in Heaven for having someone smart enough to invent a GPS navigational system for a guide. That was a huge asset. As we found ourselves leaving the city and climbing, literally, to new altitudes, we started to relax into our new awareness of the differences in our culture.

Our first disagreement along the way was when and where to stop for food and water. I understood after a conversation with him that he was actually worried about my welfare, which is something I seldom even consider for myself. He said that if he had been by himself, he would not have hesitated to get out at some of the places that looked a bit, as he says, shady and congested, but because I was with him he was choosing differently. It was a considerate way to demonstrate how he feels and sees me, being my protector in a place that was foreign to us. I was frustrated before he spoke and, afterwards, felt kind of cherished. It's funny how we are always learning about each other, especially in stressful situations, and we just find and build a newness and awareness in each other. Our life is such a great challenge, and the journeys we have together are the best lessons to date.

We got to our destination eventually and (not by coincidence) we ended up right smack dab in the middle of SMA. To say it was amazing is an understatement! (AMAZING IS A VERY POWERFUL WORD)! I could not believe or, for a better word, conceive the beauty of this hidden treasure of a place tucked into the mountains of such vast rawness! The whole place was like a starburst of colour and emotion and smells and sights like nothing I could have ever imagined! It only got better as the week progressed. Both Joe and I had interesting reactions to our environment. Like the very first time I laid eyes on the massive Church in the town square. How my eyes just started leaking! I was taken aback by the man-made cathedral. Or the personal experience my partner shared with me upon entering another building. For my partner to even have a desire to discuss his private feelings with me about how this made him feel was a huge deal. The place was, and is, magical. We experienced slow-paced, fine dining with whole foods and rich hearts. We had the best tour guides, as the friends we stayed with had fallen in love with SMA and the culture years ago and now reside there for three months of the year. We experienced educational and cultural tours and home-cooked food, history lessons, and great walks and treks.

I do want to say that, again, action is always the truth. We were out for a walk one day and my friend and I were witness to a baptism - not just one baby, but five, all dressed up in white gowns, with family all around them. Also, on another day we walked in behind a Quinceanera (a coming-out party for a 16-year-old girl). She was dressed in a brightly-coloured, orange wedding dress. She had attendants and little flower girls. They were so beautiful and full of love and tradition and were taking this very seriously.

On Sunday, my partner spotted a Holy Sister of the Catholic Church selling religious articles at the church courtyard. I made a bee-line straight to her and asked another man who spoke broken English if she would be so kind as to give me a blessing. She immediately directed me to come and stand in front of her behind the modest table where she was working. She started speaking her beautiful Spanish a mile a minute; then she grabbed a water bottle, opened it up, and started sharing the water, liberally making the sign of the cross. It was so powerful, it felt like she physically removed my heart, gave it a shake-out like you would a mat, and put it back inside me. With gratitude and love and an instant re-action to the action she so lovingly and unconditionally gave me, I did what I always do in these moments. I grabbed her and gave her a bear hug. I could feel this was foreign to her, but she received it with the same respect and unspoken God-language to which we all are connected. I had tears streaming down my cheeks as I reconnected with Joe and our friends, and, as always, I shared my blessing with my partner. He was moved as well.

One night, we were walking around the square and it was feeling so blissfully peaceful. As I opened myself to witness the world around me, I saw hundreds of gentle souls coming together. Families brought their own picnics and small children played with toys. It seemed the bands were playing in segmented areas, all different music, but all united in a beautifully orchestrated connection. It was the most festive, happy, angelic sound. The Cathedral Church, constructed with love and pride, seemed to dance with light and a gentle, subliminally illuminating, consistent energy. Vendors were busy selling all kinds of things. There were the traditional Mexican bride and groom paper mache actors on very high stilts having fun with the crowd.

I just wanted to paint you a picture so I could lead you into this thought. The peace of the people, the love that was unspoken, the lack of fear in that crowd held my heart captive. They had nothing special and everything that mattered in the moments they were creating together. There was no violence or judgment. Laughter and happiness spoke louder than I have ever witnessed. It was pure heavenly bliss. It was like a giant angel had her arms around that mountain town and the people in it. It's like they had a secret more powerful than any words. That experience, because I was open to see with my heart, was God's true essence, and the experience and memory will leave me humbled and thankful (fuel for my soul tank) for days that have more rain than sunshine in my life.

I can honestly say that I have hundreds of these kinds of stories and experiences. I am drawn to people and people are drawn to me. I have made this my life's purpose. Some days when I am a tad tired or cranky or maybe did not catch a full night's sleep, I draw on one of these experiences and it reminds me full on, in my face, once again, how lucky I am to be a part of this universe and life happenings.

Energy Healing

I want to share one recent experience that is fresh in my heart and memory. I have mentioned a boss who fully believes in holistic healing and energy work. As long as I get my job done, she allows my soul work into my work space. How fortunate I am to have this to bring into my work space. One of my like-minded co-workers, who comes down pretty frequently when needing a top-up or a full-on fill of Reiki, popped down recently to sit in what we deem the Reiki seat. I can still work around the person sitting in the chair receiving what they need. She had been suffering with a sinus infection that had her pretty down and out. She has been drawn to Reiki for years, having received many treatments over the years to help her in her pregnancy and healing in other ways. She is so in tune with her body that she knows exactly what she needs and where it is going in her body. It is an instant transfer for her and she is a sponge for the Reiki. It is so refreshing to be in her innerspace, as she knows and accepts what she needs with gratitude.

Recently, we were chatting as she was receiving and she stated that ever since she came to this new office building, she had felt an energy or presence and had developed some kind of reaction or allergy and she hated the fact that she could not identify or understand what it was that she was dealing with. Being in the Reiki mode of delivering from the educated sources we are connected to, I spoke up. Now, you must understand when this happens it is not a thought, it is more like a channel. I have no time to process or filter this verbal action. My voice communicated to her that she needed to embrace this energy or alien that wanted to cause this physical reaction to her body. Instead of working against it in annoyance and even fear, accepting that, inevitably, in the end it might cause her infliction or discomfort, she actually needed to invite it into her body. In doing so, she was allowing her brilliant body to do what it was built to do, i.e. accept the foreign invasion of this culprit and build a new defense and antibody, and deal with it by creating new road maps within, navigating and re-arranging and healing her physical body to a new level of health. She completely understood this message and undertook to act on it immediately. We were able to do some healing work to address and release this energy that was affecting her core self and whole being, and she confirmed several weeks later that the presence had dissipated and she had remained free in her airways and much less congested.

I think many times if we step outside ourselves and accept the idea of spirit hosts wanting to help us be the best we can be and that there are thousands of partners in spirit who want to aid us to quicker answers to all things and all types of education we are seeking, we become a mass of wholeness in, around, and on so many levels.

I truly believe God would want his children to have softer blows of lessons learned. I know as a parent, if I could have the power to soften blows for my children, I would try to do that. I have also learned by being a parent and a human being that the fact that I have been fortunate to carry life does not give me permission to try and control it, just because I may think my lessons are better or I want to protect my children from hurt or heartache. These individual souls born here into human flesh have their own lessons bringing them learning on all levels.

The key is if they ask for guidance, help, or experience and are open to what you may have to say, that is an entirely different story. They will learn because they will choose to accept and consider the options of their choices differently.

Being a parent does not mean, in my case, that I was a good mother. In truth, I was not. I did not do the job of mothering the way a mother should or could do. I have always been a good parent, though, for the masses who come to me and ask for help or answers. In truth, we all fit in to some kind of mold and if that takes time or a lifetime, it is all valuable and all an important part of your lessons.

I think that, for me, is why God gave me all the gifts I asked for and continues to give me an abundance of them daily. I think it is simply because I asked the source of the Divine for assistance. I asked how I could rise above and see things clearer, and I have asked for gifts to help assist the people who want to rise above, as well, but may be stuck in a place they have grown past or apart from.

When I channel, my goal is to make myself available for the person for whom I am channeling. I do work with many clients on clearing pain, heartache, past soul scar tissue, and present heart scar tissue by a means of energy extraction work, helping them step by step and allowing them the power to cut the cords and claim personal freedom.

I am telling you this because for me, my future really is "being dedicating daily to being accountable in loving presence." It is the only reality I have to work with. If I work on choosing to be more present, then I witness the manifestation of my actions. My attitude creates gratitude. These ingredients create happiness in my state of mind, body, and soul.

This takes commitment. It takes a tough alligator skin so that you can deflect negativity from your innerspace (from the inside out instead of the outside in).

This is the most important thing you can do for you. Live your moments like they are your future, so when you get to the future, you are living the moments you have predestined and created in positive light with love at the root of the creation.

The Violet Breath

Speaking of alligator skin reminds me of another longtime friend who actually lives in Louisiana. She puts a smile on my face. Miriam's skin is not like an alligator, although I am sure she has run into a few in her neck of the woods, or in this case it may be more appropriate to say swamp! She reminds me more of a steel magnolia. Beautiful and incredibly talented, she has many gifts to offer including being a stellar cook and baker. She is an artist and she writes poetry, plays piano, and has a beautiful singing voice. She is a master at many crafts and teaches beautiful lessons of Theology through historical facts. She loves all nations and speaks several languages, including understanding and sharing with the universe the love language of the human soul. She is unique in thought and fashion and splashes her very own style and colour all over the world she lives in. I value her opinion as she critiques with love and grace. I have become more feminine over the years we have shared together, as she teaches me how to use prettier words to have powerful effect.

Before sharing her gift of poetry, I would like to go into a bit of information about something I use every day, and truly this has become second nature to me. It is a healing breath that I learned during my Reiki training. I believe I received this gift from the Divine. I also am guided in how to visualize this violet breath and to send it where it is needed. My Master was so good at explaining in detail how this breath works and the power of its healing, and yet, somehow it has taken on a life of its own!

I have a description to share. I close my eyes and see the beautiful red energy of earth. I visualize my kundalini chakra, and then from my crown I visualize the universal blue energy uniting the energies through my breath in the middle of my solar plexus chakra. With the two colours mixing together, they become an iridescent, brilliant violet colour. I then put my hands together and release this sacred breath into the Universe. Its destiny has a healing power of its own.

My wise Sage and teacher once shared with me that the love and energy you send to a specific person, if it is not received or accepted, is never, ever wasted. It just floats like a dandelion feather to the next person or place that needs what it has to offer and is open to receiving it. And what is it offering? Pure love and healing energy! I am in love with this healing breath so much that it is as much a part of me as breathing every day!

I was so touched that this dear heart was inspired from her innerspace and felt a calling to capture her experience of violet breath in words. With her permission, of course, she has allowed me to share it with you, and I do so in the next section of this book. I hope it lights a fire in your heart and soul like it did for me the very first time I read it.

Inspired by Friends

I Lose my Way

Violet is the colour
She breathes
and sends with
Healing on its wings
to catch a fair wind
that knows my name,
my particular space.

But the wind follows
another way
toward another soul

I smile as I muse,
"Where did it land?
Uzbekistan- Yes!"
Alighting upon one there
His skin pricks
His veins warm
as it seeps towards his soul.

Yet she breathed for me.
It is sufficient
for the Healer
for the Receiver
and
for the Knower
that love is never wasted.

Miriam C. E. Overton

Inter-Connection

I would very much like to talk about inter-connection at this point in this Innerspace journey you have all come along on with me. I wanted to say, firstly, from the bottom of my toes to the top of my crown, that I am very blessed to have enjoyed your company and the valuable time you have given to me and yourself in reading along, and maybe even relating to some of the history or life lessons.

My sole purpose was one of love and light and simplicity. If I could wish something for everyone, it would be to fall in love with their complete and beautiful whole package, both on a physical, as well as on a soul level. I would wish them peace and love and light and grace. My wish is for people to heal and to grow and to become powerful in all their personal choices.

In retrospect, I decided after discussion with one of my soul sisters, to ask for some inter-connection and personal thoughts from a few clients and an assortment of relationships over my years of residing on this planet and the interaction we have shared.

The following messages reflect to some degree what I thought would be written by them in describing their experience with the connection, but I must say, the overwhelming love, support, and authenticity of what they have come to gain and the truth in the healings and choices for them, and for me, have been truly astounding. Most people do not receive these kinds of treasures while still living, and this encourages me to carry on and to continue to love one heart at a time and be open for any person who comes into my awareness.

From Lilly:

"How I met Tracey and ended up with this wonderful connection of unconditional love and respect we have between us...

"I have had an acquaintance with Tracey for many years through one of the companies we did business with. She was one of two people I would speak to whenever I had to call that company. Tracey was always a very happy, positive and outgoing person to speak to on the phone. No matter what kind of day she was having, she always found a way to make it a good conversation. She was so good at finding some thread of sunshine on a rainy day.

"The day that relationship went from just an acquaintance to something bigger was on February 2nd, 2010. I was going through some very difficult times in my life. I was slowly losing my mother (my rock, my one and only person I could tell everything to) to a devastating cancer. Along with that, I was going through the deepest depression I had ever experienced; the kind of depression that so many people have, but can't explain why or how or what causes it. It just happens.

On that February day, I was in such a bad state, crying and sobbing for so long that my whole body ached. My heart was broken and I didn't know what to do or how to fix it. At that moment, I had an overwhelming urge to get out of bed, go down to my home office, pick up the phone, and call Tracey. Someone in my ear was telling me to call Tracey. The weird thing was that I was able to dial her number off by heart. I didn't need to look up her phone number; it just came to me. Tracey (and not her co-worker) picked up the phone, and at that moment all my emotions flooded out to her. She allowed me to do that and was there to listen, love, and support me. She gave me her time to just let me cry and grieve and let go of all my heartaches in that phone call. When I got off the phone, a real sense of calm and peace came over me. I got dressed and made a nice dinner for my family that night. (I hadn't done that very often over those last few months.) That day, Tracey helped me see that there are things bigger than all of us out there. We just need to listen to our hearts and souls and follow what they are telling us. That day, someone whispered into my ear and told me to call Tracey. I can only tell you that no one was home with me at the time, but I had the strongest push to obey that voice and I am so happy I did!

"Six years later, our relationship has grown and strengthened so much. Tracey helped me go through the difficult times of watching my mother slip away in 2011. We would have many talks and Tracey would tell me that my mama was in the room, wearing a specific outfit or piece of jewelry. I found that to be both encouraging and calming in my soul, to know my mama was with me more now in her spiritual state than she was able to be in her physical form. She continues to help me navigate through some tragic and devastating times, but she always does it without hesitation and with total love and support in her heart.

"We love each other unconditionally and respect each other's space and boundaries. We are so connected that some days, she knows I'm having a rough day and, out of the blue, the phone rings or the e-mail comes and it is Tracey connecting with me, letting me know I'm in her heart that day. I think I have done the same for her, too, on her bad days. We allow each other to unleash and clear out frustrations and fears, then move on with our day in good ways. Our bond is strong, and I am so grateful and blessed to have found that TRUE SOULMATE. Sadly, not many people can say that in their lifetime. I cherish our friendship every day and believe that we will have that connection forever."

From a friend and soul student:

"I met Tracey on April 4th, 2001. That was the day we became co-workers. I went into the lunchroom to make a cup of tea and she was sitting at one of the tables. We started talking and 15 years later, we still haven't run out of things to say. Tracey always makes herself available to anyone who wants to talk. They go to her for advice, to vent, or sometimes just to sit beside her to absorb her healing presence. During the years of our friendship I have noticed that, depending on the subject, Tracey stops being Tracey, and someone with the wisdom of the ages takes her place. I'm not saying she goes into a trance and an apparition with a different voice starts speaking. It's Tracey's voice and she is doing the talking, but the thoughts that are being articulated flow seamlessly and are clearly being provided by some higher power. She has even said, 'I don't have to think; the words just come out.' I have learned a lot from this wise old sage, whoever he or she may be.

"When Tracey started training to become a Reiki Healer, I had never even heard of it. As she started to explain the concept, I became fascinated, although I must admit, a bit skeptical. She booked me for a session and I was a little unsure of what to expect. What was I supposed to feel during and, more importantly, after the treatment? Would this be a life-changing experience, or worse, what if nothing at all happened? Tracey began the session while soft music played in the background. As I lay there, I felt myself relaxing - just relaxing, nothing more. Near the end of the treatment, Tracey asked if there was anyone on my mind who had passed on. The first person who came to my mind was my paternal grandmother and I told her this. She said, 'No. The person standing beside me is a man.' 'Standing beside you????' I thought. 'Okay......,' she continued. 'He is kind of short and has the most brilliant blue eyes.' Immediately I said, 'My dad. He died in 1979.' She then said, 'There are tears in his eyes. He wants to say he is sorry for all the pain he caused you during your childhood and that he is around you all the time.' Tracey did know that my father had passed on, but I had never described what he looked like, so I was a little taken aback, but the thing that convinced me that she had this incredible gift was after the session when we were walking out of the Reiki room. She turned to me and said, 'I know this is going to sound weird, but he didn't have any teeth.' I could not believe it! My father had his own teeth removed and replaced with dentures several years before he died. He very seldom ever wore them because they were ill fitting and hurt his mouth.

"Realizing that my father had been watching over me brought me much closer to him in death than I ever was when he was alive. He had been a soldier fighting on the front lines in WWII. That generation was taught not to talk about the war, so they had to deal with what today would be called post-traumatic stress disorder. His remedy was the bottle and he became an abusive alcoholic. My mother had to take the brunt of his rage when he was drunk and, needless to say, my siblings and I never bonded with him. After he died, I really didn't think about him that often, but I knew he couldn't help what he had become and I didn't blame him. He was living in a nightmare, trying to deal with memories that no human should have to relive over and over again.

"Tracey opened the door to spirituality for me that day and it was life changing. I have never looked at the world the same since. I am much more open now and understand that just because you can't see something doesn't mean it isn't there. There are many more instances of how she has brought enlightenment to my life, but that would be another whole chapter."

From Janni:

"So many thank you's to you, Tracey. You truly are a gift that keeps on giving and giving. When I was told a few years ago that you were 'different' in an amazing kind of way and that I must meet you, I had no idea that my life would be forever changed as a result of that meeting. Through your pure intent and truthful words, you continually help me to grow on a soul level. The connection we have transcends all physical boundaries. I am infinitely grateful for our deepening friendship and for all that you bring to the world. The main underlying theme that you have helped me to fully understand is Acceptance.

"I can apply the simple yet profound principle by simply loving what is. I believe we are here to experience the experience and not focus only on the outcome because as soon as that outcome is achieved, then another experience arises and so it continues. We seem to be growing together, uplifting each other on our journey, and have a deep knowing in our hearts that yes, we all make a difference. Thank you for being you and being there!

"With Love and gratitude."

From Miriam:

"Some years ago, I lost my mother, my marriage, and my home in a short span of a few months. My seemingly perfect life had been wiped off the map. In the wreckage of what was, I had no idea how to move forward, how to rebuild, how to be happy. Tracey was a constant companion during those dark days - her wisdom, strength and cheer were often the only light I could see.

"She'd tell me that happiness was a choice, that all of what we are or will be is because we choose it. Tracey and I have the kind of friendship where we are free to disagree with one another - without affecting the deep respect and genuine affection we have for one another. So the very notion that I was choosing to be unhappy seemed utterly ridiculous! I let her know as much. Who would choose to live through what befell me and who would choose to be so thoroughly miserable?

"That isn't to say I didn't try to be happy. I did. And the trying mattered. I did not often succeed in those days, but I kept trying. I chose, I failed, I chose, I failed... and then one morning, years later, while picking berries in my garden, I paused and realized I was happy, truly happy. It had snuck up on me.

The choosing mattered... It still matters. I still have to choose - daily! Sometimes, I still fall flat on my face. I still fail sometimes, but I keep choosing. And I am so grateful Tracey never gave up, never let me get away with wallowing for long."

From Melody:

"My white witch - That's what I call her. She has the heart of an angel and the talents of a witch. She uses her talents only for the good of others, so definitely white witch! I've known her for 21+ years. I've seen her hit the top of the mountain and the pit of the valley. In both situations, she has nothing but love in her heart for others and the desire to please. She is the one constant friend in my life and I will never let go of her. Friends come in and out of your life as situations change and years go by. Not this one! You don't let go of this girl. She is a true friend like no other. She knows I'm a full-on skeptic when it comes to her powers, but she doesn't let it bother her; she just does what she needs to do and I let her because that's who she is and I love her. We've shared some tears over the years and laughed so hard we couldn't breathe. We've told each other our deepest secrets and taught each other stuff we didn't even think we needed to know. We've helped each other out over the years. We've walked hundreds of miles together and I'm afraid to tally the amount of ice cream we've shared (it's ridiculous but it was necessary). Nonetheless, she is MY white witch and I'm so proud to see her finally write this book!"

From Ana:

"There is a definitive moment in a person's life when they become acutely aware of the fact that they found their soul mate. I'm not talking about the person they'll spend the rest of their days waking up to each morning. I'm talking about the awkward person you didn't like who forced themselves into your life day by day, little by little, with your not even knowing then that this would change your life forever. So, to that awkward person, my best friend:

"Thank you for being you and for letting me be me. Thank you for letting me feel so much like myself when I'm with you. Thank you for not making me wear any masks or put on any fronts. Thank you for sharing in my happiest moments, and for genuinely feeling the same; for listening to my saddest stories and radiating compassion and empathy from wherever you are. Thank you for being the person in whom I want to confide.

"Thank you for being the most beautiful person, inside and out. Thank you for making the world a better place, just by being in it. Thank you for making colors a little brighter, sunshine a little warmer, and hugs a little better. Thank you for loving more fiercely than anyone I know. Thank you for defining selflessness, always putting others before yourself; you are going to change the world just as much as you have changed mine.

"Thank you for the laughs, for the cries, and for everything in between. Thank you for being my rock, my anchor; for keeping me grounded when I feel like I might otherwise blow away. Thank you for all of the things you do, big and small. Thank you for always knowing what to say and for being one of life's best teachers. Thank you for making fun of me when I deserve it, and for loving me when I don't. Thank you for staying constant in a world full of change, and for keeping some normalcy in a world full of chaos.

"Thank you for laughing as hard as we have over the years and supporting me over my cries. Thank you for setting the bar so high and making it impossible to find another friend as good as you. Thank you for making the thirty long years we have been friends feel like they just began yesterday and for giving me enough memories to last a lifetime, but not ending there. Thank you for loving me. Thank you for the absolute privilege and honor of being able to call you my best friend; thank you for being my person. Thank you for giving me these reasons, and a million more, to be thankful.

"Forever and Always"

From Billy and Tammie:

"As I sit here at 46 years old and reflect back on my life, it is amazing and humbling to really take a look at all the events and people who have come and gone and are still a part of this journey we call life! The biggest blessing I have received is being able to share this journey with my awesome wife, Tammie. A few years ago through some turns of events, Tammie and I had the pleasure of meeting Tracey. At the time I was very skeptical, or maybe a little apprehensive, about having a healing session with Tracey, which she picked up on very quickly I might add! Due to my being a little nervous, Tammie and I went as a couple.

"The very first experience with Tracey totally blew my mind! The fact that she could mediate between my father and me and some other special people in our past has truly helped Tammie and me deal with some of the feelings we had about our loved ones who have passed and to whom we never got to say goodbye. Knowing that they are truly happy and safe where they are has helped us greatly. Through spirit and Tracey's gift, she has helped us strengthen an already strong marriage with her guidance and reassurance that the path of life we are on is the exact path we are supposed to be on. Tracey has helped us in so many ways, one of the biggest being her ability to listen and guide us through some major decisions we were faced with in one of our companies. She gave us the reassurance that the decisions we were making were for our benefit, and that the people we thought we would affect in the end would also be fine. It is always amazing that she would ask, 'Have you thought of this?' And we would look at each other and laugh and say, 'Yes. That is exactly what we were talking about on the way here.'

"Another thing she has been instrumental in is helping us realize is that people who have come in and out of our lives in the past were there at that time for a reason, and their actions were for their own purpose; that we have to love everyone where they are at; and that their future choices are not ours to choose. This has truly helped me look at things and people in our lives through a different set of eyes. Tracey has become a truly blessed friend in our lives, and we will continue to be honoured to have her in our lives wherever the journey takes us.

"Much love."

From Jacqui:

"My connection with Tracey is one of many threads through the universal life force. We have known each other for many, many years. We first met at the baseball field through my mum, and I also babysat Tracey's step-daughters during my teens, but we reconnected when we started working together. I think of Tracey as a teacher, mentor and, most of all, my friend. She has reminded me to trust in myself. She has given me confidence in my abilities, and is always there when I need a friend who understands what I am saying. We connect through our Reiki. We help each other when we can and we are there for each other at the right times. Tracey helped me with my long days at work during my pregnancies, and I truly believe that with Tracey's help, our energy helped my lovely Raven be who she is today: healthy, strong, and a sponge for information and sensory input. I believe that we gave Raven the best start she could ever have, and she has thrived and astounded all who meet her. For this I am eternally grateful. Tracey is the bundle of energy who tells it like it is and the bundle of love that makes my heart smile."

Note from Tracey:

Jacqui was the first person with whom I felt comfortable enough to share my first draft of this book." She spent time and energy looking over and advising as well as amending some of my atrocious spelling and grammar. I trusted her, as she is a wise sage witch with a degree of insight that far surpasses even her understanding! Love her and love that she believed in the purpose of the message in this book.

Love, Tracey

From Marla:

"My first meeting with Tracey was on the phone. She called to see if I would teach Reiki to her. Some good friends of hers had gifted her the funds to learn Reiki. The daughter of one of those friends was friends with my daughter, and so Tracey and I found each other.

"She was jumping out of her skin excited, one step away from fear and ready to learn when she arrived at my house. We hugged each other and she shed a few tears. I was a little overwhelmed with this lady's exuberance, and when she humbly gifted me with a CD she had recorded, I was very grateful and moved that she would share something so personal at our first meeting. The CD contained Christian music, and I did my best to not be judgmental. I realized that Tracey was devoted to her religion, and I wondered if we would be able to accept each other's passionate beliefs. I honestly thanked her and thought it was impressive that she had recorded her songs. The cover of the CD was beautiful and the title, 'Traces of the Heart' I loved. I thought to myself, 'Too bad it's all about religion.' I put it on a shelf with my other CD's and forgot about it, or at least tried to.

"We met several times for Reiki teachings and just for fun, and each time my love and like for Tracey grew. We had so many amazing healing experiences together. One in particular stands out. During Reiki II training we learn to send Reiki into the past, and we were both sending to Tracey at a time that had been photographed. She was a toddler in a pretty little dress and was peeking out of a car window. I got the impression she was on: full of beans and sparkling.

"It was a very powerful sending. There was so much Reiki flowing into this little one. I was so aware of my adult hands on this little being. So much Reiki on her throat and I heard the words, 'She is going to need her voice to be strong.'

"There was more Reiki Energy than I had ever felt before going to her and through her for others to heal. The healing went very deep and far into the past and just kept flowing. Now, I saw her in my mind's eye: a toddler lying on her back with two fingers in her mouth, sleeping. I kept thinking that this was so much Reiki for a little one. I was aware in a profound way of just how precious each little being is and that this healing energy was going out to all the precious little ones on this earth through Tracey. On her little belly I felt hunger and suffering and layers upon layers of Reiki and the words, 'Tracey is a healer. It's not what she does; it's who she is.'

"This brings me back to that CD that had gathered a full layer of dust. I was housecleaning one day and thought, 'I love and care about Tracey. It's about time I listen to her CD.' I playfully thought, 'I can put it on while I vacuum.' (I can hear you laughing, Tracey!) Don't get me wrong, I love music. I cannot carry a tune and am amazed when people can sing. I was having problems with the religious theme. I respect everyone's choice of spiritual practice, as well as the choice to not have one. I had pulled away from any structured religion when I was young. It's not that I had any bad experiences; it just didn't fit me. My spiritual practice is inspired by nature and fills me with clear flowing love, compassion, and peace. I was worried about what I would say to Tracey if I didn't like her CD.

"Well, I put it on and pushed play and continued vacuuming.

Then I heard her voice! I didn't know what the words were. I literally dropped in a chair, with a river of tears that instantly began running down my face, and listened to something that filled me with love and beauty. My words cannot explain how blown away I was by the effect that her beautiful singing had on me, and even now when I listen to the CD or am lucky enough to hear her sing in person, it still blows me away and fills me with love and beauty.

"My concerns about our differences in our spiritual beliefs or anything else are not what is important. Our beautiful experiences, deep conversations, many laughs, and much love and respect are what matters.

"Over the years I have come to know that Tracey, one way or another, has this loving effect on just about everyone who is as blessed as I am to have this earth angel in our lives.

"With love and light from your teacher, your student, Marla."

Conclusion

A Soul-Kissed Saturday

Saturday, June 4th, 2016 started out like any other Saturday. Joe and I got up pretty early as we had a meeting to attend. The meeting was an annual board meeting that happens usually the first Saturday in June. It went smoothly, as it does every year. We are blessed to have such committed, caring people dedicated to living and loving our communal home.

The meeting was adjourned at 12:00 noon, and then we got on the bike and Joe asked me where I would like to have lunch. I mentioned a particular restaurant where they hand-dip chicken fingers and have deep-fried Wisconsin cheese curds...honestly, a heart-clogging, amazing, delectable experience! I was a little disappointed when the bike and the rider headed to Croswell to a different establishment; however, I do enjoy their breakfast biscuit sandwich, so soon settled into the seat behind the driver on the bike.

We arrived safely and were sitting enjoying our meal when we overheard a conversation behind us. The conversation was an employee asking a lady how her book was coming and how many words she had completed. She answered him and carried on. Joe just looked at me with that don't you even dare look. We sat in silence, enjoying the sunshine coming through the window. Joe got up to use the facilities, and I got up to introduce myself to the lady behind us!

I remember her face shining like the sun and her eyes sparkling. After sharing a few words with her, she invited both of us to sit down with her. She shared very valuable information with us. She had had a long-time dream of becoming a writer and has had quite a long successful career. The book she was working on at that time would be her sixth publishing accomplishment. Joe once again had no idea that he was the instrument in this divine connection. We were at the stage where we were trying to gain knowledge and direction on how to proceed with this project. We both left the restaurant with gratitude, each in a different kind of thought and with a whole new perspective.

The day got better!

We got back home and decided that it was such a grand day, we would take out the boat and spend some time on it together, just the two of us. I will not speak for Joe, but the encounter I had just experienced left me in a state of awe. This author kindly gave us two books and had written personal messages in them. I took one along and every time I opened the book to a page (four times consecutively), it opened to a page that was titled, "Keeping it Simple." What a powerful message for me!

We were enjoying the day on the water in our own "Innerspace" - Joe finding peace and contentment in the instruments on the boat and just relaxing in his element; me in reflection of the day, my life, this project in which I had become absorbed.

We arrived at our destination, docked our boat, and proceeded to walk into town together. It was a perfect afternoon, around 3:30 p.m., and we decided to go into a little place and order a cold draft beer and a take-out pizza. We sat at the bar to have a rest and enjoy our cold beverage. We sat beside a couple at the bar and started to have a chat about the day, and just like that, we had an instant connection. We exchanged names and small talk and then when we were getting ready to leave, the woman and I got into a conversation about healing work and discovered we had travelled a similar path in life, both receiving Reiki Master Teacher. We hugged and connected immediately to the passion we have been called to.

We went our separate ways and all I could do walking back to the boat to go back home was smile from ear to ear, knowing that I had been given several soul gifts this day! It so happens in awareness, that opportunity is always there for me personally to have the experience in these golden nuggets. In "my reflection" this soul-kissed day, I was the receiver of messages from the forces I work with daily and do not visually see. These two women, "spiritually different" but following the calling in their hearts, were given to me as gifts in the connections and the bond of love I felt from them. More often than not, these connections feed and validate the missions we are on to develop the love we have in our own souls and then choose to share it with the world. On that soul-kissed Saturday, that is exactly how it was for me!

Fascinating to me on that day was the fact that these two worlds - my Christian roots and my Reiki roots - my Jesus and my Mikao Usui - both met at my heart through two different women on the same day. Both of these women demonstrated unconditional love and acceptance for others. How much more awesome can a day get! By means of different forms of dedicated, committed practice, both women love the world about which they have been called to teach, deeply feeling their calling and listening to the sounds and voices in their hearts.

To say this timing was not divine intervention to me is simply not the truth. It was a powerful awareness that when you are called, it is not accidental. It is a calling that registers and brings forth the lessons of the calling, bringing the truth home with clarity. I know I need to move forward and I know there is room for all of us. I know I need to be kind and tolerant. I know I need to judge less and listen more. I know I need to take the wisdom of the roots and Masters I have been given and know they, too, have love and room in their beings for each other. With respect and wisdom, the connection just becomes that much more intricately beautiful!

A Journey of Love and Life

As I reflect and ponder all the experiences that have come to pass for me, I just know that I am beyond blessed to have had these lessons. They have taught me to rise above and connect with combined life forces in spirit and in flesh, as we all work together united as one loving being. Don't forget, ever - you still get to keep your identity.

I see myself with my finished book in my hand, standing in a room just like my partner's vision board. I feel the love as thick as syrup. It smells sweet and it feels wonderful. I see people being fed by the untapped universal love, and it is pouring into their hearts. I see the beautiful cover and feel Beverly smiling and loving all the people who pick the book up and imagine their own spirit guides in the picture. I see people soaking it all in and, most importantly, I see people in front of my very own blue eyes actually taking the time to fall in love with the beauty within their own innerspace.

After all, there is room in this universal space for all of us. We all have gifts to bring to the massive table laid out for us. In turn, we all get to share the wealth that multiplies in the masses with whom we are entwined. We collectively get to choose every day, paying it all forward for the cause and effects of love.

I have had many lifetimes, many deaths, and many births in this short almost 60-year journey. I have one wish every day for the millions who struggle with the hollowness inside their innerspace. That wish would be to warm them up, wake them up, and show them by the action of love that they are worth finding, and cultivating, and loving the journey and ride they are on by seizing their moments in this lifetime. Yes, this takes commitment, time invested, and time alone to really take the moments in your day to commit to yourselves, in love and action. This takes respecting your own personal boundaries! In those selected moments, become aware and accountable. It takes a kind, loving heart within to forget and to forgive what some people may not think is even forgivable. The rewards for themselves are finally, "an understanding of true acceptance within and peace around them."

I promise if you do this, if you decide to love the very being you were born into, accept who it is and love it the way you love others, you will then honestly and truly fall in love with your own being. This love grows quickly as it is healthy and wholesome. It feeds and nurses you inside and grows healthy shoots that encompass your whole being with an understanding and an acceptance that you, indeed, are perfect in the exact state you are in, in the exact moment you are living.

I think you are so worth it! It is so awesome to look into other beings' eyes and register the love they have in the light that shines through them for themselves and for the world that is theirs around them. After all, the light in someone else's eyes is merely a reflection of the soul within your own innerspace.

Be kind to yourself, give yourself some credit, and love yourself beyond what you have been comfortable with. In truth, you only have you. If you can make a difference to you, just think of the possibilities that would bring to your world around you! Keep yourself happy and the world around you will be much brighter, even on the rainy days. Quite honestly, you don't even pay the rain any mind when sunshine resides in your heart every day!

I do promise you all to connect with you on your journey of love and life. I will invite you and carry all of you in my heart with love! My soul heart has many rooms in it and they are all waiting to collectively gather you all in. Together, we will be in communion, and, together, we will make a difference.

White light and love be with you always!